Chanhassen
A Centennial History

CHANHASSEN
A Centennial History

Daniel John Hoisington

City of Chanhassen

This book is dedicated
to
Rebecca Grace Hoisington
and
Daniel Aaron Hoisington

Fathers have many dreams for their daughters and sons.
If I had only one wish for them,
it would be that they may have children like mine.

Copyright © by City of Chanhassen, Minnesota. All rights reserved. No part of this book may be used or reproduced in any manner whatsoever without written permission except in the case of brief quotations embodied in critical articles or reviews.

Printed by The Press, Banta Corporation, Chanhassen, Minnesota.
Type set in ITC Galliard.

Hoisington, Daniel John.
Chanhassen: A Centennial History
    Bibliography: p.
    Includes index.

1. Chanhassen (MN)—History. 2. Chanhassen (MN)—History—Pictorial works. I. Title.

ISBN 1-889020-03-6
Library of Congress Catalog Card Number 96-85268
First Edition: July 1996

Table of Contents

Preface...7

Introduction...9

Chapter One...12
First Settlers

Chapter Two...20
A More Desirable Community

Chapter Three...42
Divisions

Chapter Four...60
An American Schwarzwald

Chapter Five...84
The Garden Spot of the World

Chapter Six...104
Hot Days, Cold Nights, Hard Work

Chapter Seven...114
"A Village Small and Fair"

Chapter Eight...142
Rituals

Chapter Nine...156
Shakers and Movers

Chapter Ten...174
One Chanhassen

Index...188

Bibliographic Notes...190

Acknowledgments...192

Preface

Chanhassen's centennial gives us all an opportunity to reflect on our heritage and the men and women who shaped our community. We owe a great deal to the early pioneers who faced many challenges in their quest to establish a community. Their foresight and courage formed Chanhassen into the vibrant and progressive city that it is today.

In the words of Oliver Wendell Holmes, Jr., "When I want to understand what is happening today or try to decide what will happen tomorrow, I look back." I can only hope that one hundred years from now, residents will be proud of our accomplishments and how we have shaped the community for future generations.

—Mayor Donald J. Chmiel

Introduction

The history of Chanhassen is close at hand. During my research for this book, I talked with many older Chanhassen residents who had known the men and women who founded the village one hundred years ago. Henry James called it the visitable past—the past connected by a living presence, "the marks and signs of a world we may reach over to as by making a long arm we grasp an object at the other end of the table."

When we reach over that table, what wisdom can we take? Local history books fall into many traps. Sometimes the past is enshrined as "the good old days," an approach that is especially appealing to a community that has seen the dramatic growth of Chanhassen. The opposite pitfall is to see the changes as the simple march of progress. A new, bigger building replaces the old. A simple country hamlet becomes a major suburb.

The lesson that I learned in the past year is that Chanhassen has been shaped by the choices of its people. A community becomes what its people want it to be.

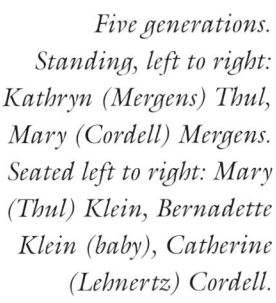

Five generations. Standing, left to right: Kathryn (Mergens) Thul, Mary (Cordell) Mergens. Seated left to right: Mary (Thul) Klein, Bernadette Klein (baby), Catherine (Lehnertz) Cordell.

The Northampton Colony came from western Massachusetts. Even in their settlement patterns, they chose to come as a group rather than as separate individuals. Although the initial dream failed and the colony broke up, the Powers, Lymans and Aspdens continued to see the township from the perspective of the New England village —ambitious farmers, driven to improvements, moral, Protestant, temperance people who started clubs, went to church, and served on township boards. They voted Republican.

The Dutch and German settlers who populated the northeast quarter of the township were inspired by the leadership of Father Magnus Mayr who argued that German Catholics were threatened by the pervasive culture of America. Mayr, who helped form St. Hubert's Parish, insisted that his followers set themselves apart. Their community was centered almost completely around their cultural and spiritual heritage. Village life began and ended at the church.

In the late 1950s and early 1960s, a new vision swept into town led by men who served in World War II. The ambitious dreams of Herbert Bloomberg and Mayor Eugene Coulter saw a town that eliminated the two distinct worlds of the township and the village. Instead of a sleepy country hamlet, they saw Chanhassen as the "Frontier Village." Few towns in Minnesota have adopted such a single-minded motif.

The most recent choices were taken in response to the sprawl of the metropolitan area from the 1960s to the present. The township and village merged into one entity following annexation battles. Overnight, Chanhassen became the largest city in Carver County. A new generation of leadership, many of them newly-transplanted to town, promoted a vision of a central downtown district that would give the city a distinct identity from the surrounding commuter suburbs. To a remarkable extent, that has been accomplished.

People have a remarkable ability to shape the community life of their choosing when working together. Rather than reading history with a sense of inevitability, Chanhassen's history forces us to accept our responsibility in the present to choose the future. It is the same question that faced the Northampton colonists, the parishioners of St. Huberts, and the civic leaders of the 1960s: What kind of community do you want?

The Centennial Book Committee has made a lasting contribution to the city. There are few primary resources for the historian. Chanhassen did not have a newspaper until recent decades. Its people were not writers but farmers. There is no community historical society.

To meet the challenge, the Committee employed several innovative techniques. They hosted several "scanning days" at City Hall during which many of the older families in town brought their cherished photographs and papers to be recorded. All were carefully scanned into a computer, catalogued, and placed on a CD-Rom for archival purposes. This process contributed most of the illustrations that you will find in this book.

The Committee conducted oral history interviews with more than fifty local residents, who graciously donated their time and memories. The tapes were carefully transcribed by a dedicated core of volunteers. The tapes and the transcriptions give a valuable resource to any future historians, recording the transition of a rural township into an important suburb.

Finally, this centennial history should not be the close of research but a beginning. There are many incidents and issues that need to be studied in greater depth than this book offers. Hopefully, the story of the city's past as told here will inspire others in their own efforts. For me, it has been a privilege to learn about this place called Chanhassen.

Chapter One
First Settlers

THE HISTORY OF CHANHASSEN BEGINS IN MANY PLACES. It begins in Germany where social unrest moved some to travel across an ocean to find a new home. It begins in western Massachusetts in small towns in the Connecticut River Valley. It begins in the halls of Congress as the United States government decided how to distribute land.

The area that we know as Chanhassen had its own history as well. Native American populations lived there for thousands of years. Their history is found in the traces of life that archaeologists recover. Research projects show evidence of habitation around Lake Susan, Minnewashta, and Lotus Lake as early as 6000 BC. It is not surprising since water provided a ready source of food. The "Big Woods" that covered the area offered game and timber.

For one hundred years, the Dakota were the primary native group, moving into the land and displacing the Iowa peoples sometime in the 1750s. They had no major villages in Carver County although the Shakopee settlement was just across the river. The Ojibway lived to the north and west.

In 1851 the treaties of Transverse de Sioux and Mendota provided a cash payment to Native Americans in return for the land, most of southern Minnesota. The money, however, went directly to the trading companies that had extended credit to the native Americans. Within weeks, settlers began staking claims. It was never a simple transition. Many tribal groups remained in the region and many of the first generation told stories of encounters with Indians.

Land

Minnesota's primary attraction was its cheap land. The treaties opened vast new territories at precisely the time that changes in Europe opened the gates of immigration. In the 1850s and 1860s, the United States government adopted a liberal land policy that made land available to the common person.

In the early years, the government offered American soldiers bounties of government land. The bounties cost the government nothing and provided an incentive for recruits and a pension for veterans. The U.S. government reformed the system between 1850 and

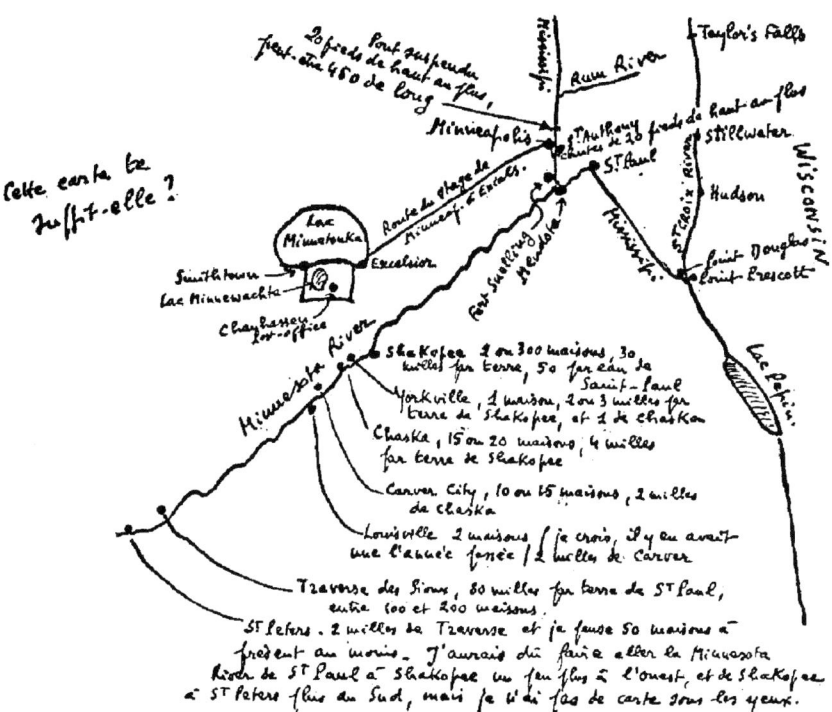

This map, drawn by Theodore Bost, shows the routes taken by the early settlers. Although some came overland by way of Minnetonka, most travelled down the Minnesota River and stopped at river ports. Note the location of Yorkville between Chaska and Shakopee.

1855, permitting the owners of military bounty lands to sell their warrants or titles. Speculators bought up thousands of titles from soldiers and their families, many of whom had no intention of ever heading to the west. The speculators entered these warrants in state and territorial land offices then resold the land at a higher price to immigrants who were eager for land. Several early settlers, Joseph Vogel and Henry Lyman, for example, purchased warrants.

The Preemption Act of 1841 opened another door for settlers. The government began auctions to sell land at a minimum price of $1.25 an acre. However, if a settler did not have enough money in the bank, they had an alternative. They could settle on the land before its sale, start a farm, and then buy the property with the profits. They were called "Squatters." Theodore Bost, an early Chanhassen settler, explained the system to his parents in Europe, writing, "I paid nothing for the land in my claim for the simple reason that the land itself didn't belong to the claimant; in the same way, if I should sell my claim, I'd ask a high price, not for the land itself, but for the right I have acquired to buy this land at a price of $1.25 an acre."

It was a gamble. If the farm failed to produce, the squatter would lose his cabin and his cleared fields. The system had its abuses. Speculators would throw up a ramshackled house and claim the land without any intention of living there. Once the property was theirs, they could resell it at a handsome profit. It helped to have a friendly neighbor. Bost noted, "I came down [to the land office] with Sarver, one of my neighbors, and we proved for each other."

The Homestead Act of 1862 reformed the system even further with the goal of eliminating these corrupt land speculation practices. It is probably the best-known way to acquire land. A homestead included up to 160 acres (a quarter section) of public land. If settlers made claim to the land, stayed on it for five straight years and improved the property, the government granted them title to the land free.

Yorkville

The Minnesota River provided the most important travel route in the first years of settlement. Although town sites had been platted for Shakopee and Chaska, a young German immigrant named John Maertz saw potential for another settlement between those two sites. Maertz was born in Darmstadt in the Grand Duchy of Hesen. He emigrated to the U.S. in the early 1840s and lived with an uncle in Baltimore, Maryland. He joined the army and was assigned to Fort Snelling in 1847. When his term of enlistment ended, Maertz remained in Minnesota and delved into land speculation.

Maertz and fellow investors laid out a town plat for the settlement of Yorkville, just to the east of Chaska. The original Yorkville settlement group included Mike Engler, Charles May, Henry Eschle, and Adam Amrhein. Maertz built a home and store, attracting other settlers. Steamboats soon began regular stops. In 1863 the military road from Fort Snelling was routed through Yorkville.

The owners of the Chaska township, living in Saint Paul, saw Yorkville as a threat. They lured several settlers to Chaska, including Mathew Iltis, Philip Henk, and Paul Faber. Yorkville faded away, although John Maertz remained in the community for many years. He died in 1900 and was buried in Mount Pleasant Cemetery.

Franz Renz was among the first investors in the Yorkville settlement. Born in Baden, Germany, Renz came to America in June 1846, looking for work in New York. Eventually, he labored on the railroads in New Hampshire then went to Boston to labor on the city's waterworks. In 1847 he headed back to New York and remained four years with a firm importing French china and glassware. He then headed to Minnesota.

John Maertz met Renz in Saint Paul and convinced him to invest in his new settlement along the Minnesota River. He did well financially. The value of his land was twice as much as the closest competi-

Joseph Vogel and Veronica Kessler were the first white couple to be married in Carver County.

Chanhassen: A Centennial History 15

Edwin Whitefield painted scenes through Minnesota during the 1850s. This painting looks across Lake Bavaria. On the far shore, a solitary cabin has been built.

tor in the 1860 state agricultural census. Renz moved to Kansas for five years but returned in 1857. He was a popular figure and was elected as the first chairman of the Board of Supervisors for Chanhassen Township. He was elected to the state legislature in 1859 and 1860 before moving to Saint Paul in 1862.

Joseph, Frank and August Vogel

The first great wave of German immigration to America came at the moment that Minnesota lands opened for sale. Why did they come? There was never one reason.

Germans read hundreds of promotional books and newspapers touting the benefits of life in America. For example, Frederick W. Bogen wrote in *The German in America, or Advice and Instruction for German Emigrants to the United States of America* (1856):

> A great blessing meets the German emigrant the moment he steps upon these shores: He comes into a free country; free from the oppression of despotism, free from privileged orders and monopolies, free from constraint in matters of belief and conscience.
>
> Everyone can travel, free and untrammeled, whither he will, and settle where he pleases. No passport is demanded, no police mingles in his affairs and hinders his movements. Before him lies the country, exhaustless in its resources, with its fruitful soil, its

productive mines, its immense products, both of vegetable and animal kingdom, a portion of which he has never before seen; its countless cities and villages, where flourish industry, commerce, and wealth.

The Vogel family landed at Yorkville in 1852. They came from Silesia, a province in eastern Germany that is now part of Poland. Joseph Vogel was born on October 18, 1824 in Ohlguth near Munsterberg. There is some question whether the Vogels lived in America for a time before they came to Carver County but the family took up the first claim in June 1852 on the bluffs to the north of Yorkville. The Vogels were squatters with no legal claim to the land. In fact, the 1851 treaties did not become official until February 24, 1853.

Just to the northwest, other Germans gathered around a lake. Although an early Minnesota historian, John Stevens, referred to them as a "colony," they each came as family groups. Since these families all came from Bavaria, many began to refer to the lake by that name.

The Kessler family—widow Barbara and six children, Heinrich, Franz, Michael, Joseph, Veronica, and Victoria—lived in a small village in Bavaria. With little opportunity to acquire farms for each of the four sons, they followed the reports about America. Several of the Kesslers' friends, namely Engelbert Schneider, Michael Ess and his sons John and Joseph, had already left for the new land and sent back glowing reports from Cincinnati, Ohio. The Kesslers decided to emigrate, selling their home and their property to pay for passage.

The Kesslers stopped in Cincinnati. At the time, the town on the Ohio River was heavily Germanic and had become the central gathering point for new immigrants. German language newspapers carried the latest reports from the territories. Cincinnati had been settled, though, for many years and all cheap land had been taken. Their friends, the Schneiders and the Ess's, had taken up farms in Michigan. The Kesslers decided to head to the new "Sulands" of Minnesota. Traveling to Saint Paul via the Ohio and Mississippi Rivers, they arrived in the region in July of 1852. The four sons, Joseph, Heinrich, Franz, and Michael filed claims on the lake. A family descendant states that the Kesslers built a large log house on Heinrich's claim near the northwest corner of the lake and lived there as they built other homes.

Tobias Ottinger arrived on May 10th, 1852. Ottinger had lived in America for several years, apparently working as a huckster for a time in Missouri and other southern states. He came from Saint Paul, loading his wagon with cooking utensils, stove, plow, some tools, and several months' food supply. It took him about a week to travel the thirty-five miles from Saint Paul to his homestead with his oxen.

Engelbert Schneider decided to join the Kesslers in Minnesota. Schneider was born in Bavaria in 1830. Some accounts suggest that he

August Vogel

Mathilda Vogel

came to America as early as 1847. He lived near Freedom, Michigan for several years where he married Anna Maurus. We know little about Anna's story although records state that she was born in Regensburg, Bavaria. In 1855, they came to Chanhassen, settling on the east side of Lake Bavaria. Michael Ess and his sons Joseph and John came with the Schneiders.

On July 15, 1854 Joseph Vogel married Veronica Kessler at the Kessler farm in Laketown—the first wedding in Carver County. Father Augustine Ravoux, a missionary, performed the ceremony. The couple had three children. Joseph and Veronica built a home, now the Bluff Creek Inn, in 1864 on land deeded to "Luther C. Clark, Musician" as warrant deed for service in the War of 1812. At the same time, August built a fine house of Chaska brick around the area now known as Vogel's Hill. Anton, John, Frank, Theresa and Anna settled nearby. Anna married Alexander Rachel, living on his claim near Lake Hazeltine. Family tradition says that Theresa moved west after marriage. John disappears from the records.

German immigrants settled in other parts of the township as well. Benedict Schmid claimed land on the northwest of Lake Minnewashta. Schmid had visited Minnesota where his brother Joseph claimed land in 1857. Benedict returned to Cincinnati to live for a year, apparently to earn enough money for his own claim.

Schmid wanted to find a wife to share life on the frontier. "I don't know how long I'm going to stay here," he wrote on June 14, 1857, "but before I go back to Minneapolis, I would like to take a wife." He

Above: Franz and Magdalena Vogel

Right: Alexander Rachel and his wife, Anna Vogel Rachel. Their farm is now part of Hazeltine Golf Course.

placed his hopes on Nancy, a distant neighbor. "I think about her a lot," he wrote. "I don't know where the idea comes from. I never talked to her and she doesn't even know me." Even farming, his real love, reminded Benedict of Nancy. After plowing a cornfield, he scribbled in his diary, "My thoughts are constantly focused on a woman. She is on my mind like a picture." When Nancy did not return his advances, he proposed to Magdalina Weimaringen. She accepted to his utter surprise. But on May 9th, 1858, he wrote, "I got a letter from Magdalina. She does not want to go to Minnesota with me. I wrote to her that I am leaving this place June 1." Schmid headed north alone.

Some families like the Rosbachs and the Paulys had farms near Lake Susan. The Paulys apparently lived in Illinois for a short time before moving to Minnesota. Both Michael Pauly and Henry Pauly had daughters that records show were born in Illinois in 1854. One source states that Nicholas and Margaretta Pauly's son, Henry, born on May 25, 1855, was the first white child born in Chanhassen.

More than half of the early settlers in the township were born in Germany. Of the 271 adults listed in the 1857 township census, they came from:

German-born: 135
New England: 48
England: 13

Only two came from southern states. Some families stopped in other states on their journey. Most listed their occupation as 'farmer.'

Engelbert Schneider was one of the early settlers along Lake Bavaria.

Left: Frederick C. Miller was born in Bavaria in 1825 and settled in Chanhassen around 1854. He married Dorothea "Charlotte" Higgens in 1851 while in Chicago. Both later moved to Eden Prairie.

Two Vogel brothers built homes near each other.

Top: August Vogel's home is located on Hwy. 101.

Below: Joseph and Veronica Vogel's home, built in 1864, is now the Bluff Creek Inn.

The land was bound to attract many more people. A government surveyor recorded his impressions of the township in his field survey notes:

> The land in this township is generally first-rate. As there is a great variety in the kinds of land lying contiguous, it is a very desirable place for farmers. Many of the settlers now in it have in their farms as much opening as they want for tillage, a sufficient quantity of timber and a large amount of excellent meadow while lakes, springs, and brooks everywhere abound. Many claims have valuable tamarack swamps on them.

A young minister in Belchertown, Massachusetts had read similar reports and talked with his friends about the prospects of settling in Minnesota.

Chapter Two
"A More Desirable Community"

On October 26, 1852, a crowd gathered in the vestry of the Methodist Church in Northampton, Massachusetts. For months, the citizens of the towns along the Connecticut River had read about the glorious prospects in the territory of Minnesota. On this day, Reverend Henry Martyn Nichols and three brothers, Levi, Porter, and Freeman Nutting, presented a plan to form a colony to travel west and settle.

The descriptions of the territory lit the imaginations on that autumn day. Reverend Freeman Nutting of South Hadley Falls described the land that awaited them. "Minnesota possesses a climate which for purity and salubrity is not equalled by any other this side of the Rocky Mountains," he wrote. "It is essentially New England...but free from our sudden changes...rendering it the most healthful climate to breathe that can be found. The land is of the first quality—unsurpassed for all purposes of agriculture by any portion of the West...having the right proportion of prairie land, oak openings, and woodlands." Nutting argued that the financial risk was minimal. "A Colony can locate themselves to their liking and have some two or three years to raise crops, make improvements, & C. without paying for their land," he wrote.

Henry Martyn Nichols, President of the Minnesota Colonization Committee

Henry Martyn Nichols, a young minister from Belchertown, Massachusetts, joined with Nutting in praise of Minnesota. He wrote to the *Northampton Courier*: "I have been led to examine the claims of this new territory, and am so well convinced of its desirableness on account of its climate, soil, and facility of access as to make arrangements for moving there next Spring." His sister, Harriet, had already moved to Minnesota in the previous year to take up a missionary post in Belle Plaine, teaching Chippewa children. Her letters encouraged his desire to head west.

Nichols had grown up in the Connecticut River Valley and held a series of ministerial posts in nearby towns. For several years Nichols

The Northampton Colony came from several towns in the Connecticut River Valley. This vista of the valley near Northampton was painted by David John Gue from the top of Mount Holyoke. From the collections of the Mount Holyoke College Art Museum.

had been frustrated by the poverty, both spiritual and financial, of his ministry. When one church steward advised him to live on faith, Nichols told him, "I must have crackers too; faith without works is dead." When the North Amherst church refused to raise a decent salary, he exclaimed, "I cannot stand it, I shall bolt. I cannot starve to death...I shall go to Amherst and preach tomorrow and tell the people that unless they pony up, I can't stay." He read about the need for missionaries in California and began studying Spanish. The lure of Minnesota proved stronger, encouraged by several meetings with Reverend Nutting.

By the close of the October meeting, the Minnesota Claim Association was organized. Nichols was elected President; Porter Nutting, Secretary and Treasurer. The finance commitee included Levi Nutting, C.S. Johnson, Charles Hayden, Freeman Nutting, and B.F. Sears. The meeting approved a set of by-laws with promises to assist the other members with their future land claims.

The Northampton Colony, as they became known, organized an advance party to travel to Minnesota to make arrangements for the main body and to scout prospective sites for permanent settlement. Throughout October, Nichols met with the Nutting brothers and Arba Cleaveland to organize their trip. They departed in mid-November, arriving in Saint Paul on December 2nd after poor roads delayed their trip between Galena and Minnesota.

The Nuttings and Nichols faced the task of selecting land for their settlement. They explored three areas—land along the Cannon River to the south, the Rum River to the north, and near Lake Minnetonka to the west. Nichols and Nutting seemed to be in agreement. Nichols wrote in his diary on January 13, 1853: "Had some conversation with Bro. Nutting about the location for our colony and with the knowledge we have at present we are both in favor of a place above rather than below Saint Paul." They took a long excursion to see Lake Minnetonka. Nutting was "perfectly enchanted with the place," Nichols wrote in mid-February.

Nichols saw the colony as more than an attempt to acquire cheap land. It meant the planting of a New England Christian sensibility to the wild and unsettled lands. "The advantages of going together in a Colony are too obvious to be mentioned. The privations and inconveniences of an isolated pioneer life will thus be overcome and instead of a seclusion of several years from society, we carry with us our own New England society," he wrote.

New England society tempered the immorality of frontier life. "It is very easy matter," Henry Nichols told his Massachusetts audience, "for an Eastern Christian to backslide in the West." Liquor was among the most dangerous temptations. A correspondent assured the prospective colonists that, "The Temperance men of the Territory are generally firm and decided, and if those who come to settle among us…exert the right influence, our Territory is safe." In this matter, they were told that the territory's Catholics could be trusted. Bishop Cretin was a sound temperance man and Saint Paul had two Catholic temperance societies.

Nutting and Nichols could not agree on the best location for the colony, although the *Saint Anthony Express* of April 15, 1853 reported that they had "both been spending some weeks at Minnetonka and seem well pleased with the locality." The final choice would await the arrival of the colonists. Nutting sent home detailed packing instructions: pack goods in large boxes, pack a bottle of water and a cup to avoid cholera, do not bring parasols. They departed Springfield, Massachusetts by train on April 6th, 1853.

The "Favorite" was a passenger and freight steamer on the Minnesota River. After the railroads were completed through Carver County, the river trade died out.

Nichols eagerly awaited the arrival of the party, frequently visiting the docks in Saint Paul. On April 19th, the Steam Boat *Time and Tide* pulled up to the docks with the first seventy-five colonists. To Nichols' chagrin, his wife was not on board. He continued to greet each arrival. "Sure enough," he recorded in his diary, "at eleven o'clock last night the S.B. Dr. Franklin came in and I found my dear wife on board nicely asleep in her berth and what could I do but lie in her arms the remainder of the night." Mrs. Nichols remembered, "Arrived in Galena at dark Friday. Staid there till Monday Eve when we started for Saint Paul…Had one of the richest finest rides that we ever enjoyed. Got to St. Paul Thursday night at twelve o'clock. We did not expect to get into Port until daylight, so I had gone to bed and was sleeping quietly, when I was awakened by some one kissing me, and starting up in fright I was clasped to my husband's arms."

The Minnesota papers caught wind of their impending arrival. The *Saint Anthony Falls Express* stated:

> A large number of Northampton colonists arrived in Saint Paul this week. Livery stables were in requisition and a steam boat chartered by the city fathers...to give the colonists an opportunity of observing the manifold and extraordinary charms of the Territory.

A choice of location had to be made. Many of the group wished to see the area that Nichols favored near Lake Minnetonka and an expedition was organized. Nichols recorded their progress:

> April 25. Started with six others, to visit the region around Lake Minnetonka. Went on, as far as Steven's mill [Minnetonka], and put up for the night...
>
> April 26. Started in two boats, with Simon Steven's for a pilot, passed up the creek into the lake, and up to the narrows at the entrance of the big lake, where we camped for the night in the open air.
>
> April 27. Started early, and went back three or four miles, from the lake. Found a splendid section of country, that pleased our whole company well. Came back to Steven's mill to spend the night.

Nutting, however, refused to commit to a location. Nichols lamented, "We are almost discouraged about selecting a good place for our colony. There are many speculators and land pirates." There was money to be made and Saint Paul was full of sharp dealers. On May 6th, the *Saint Anthony Express* printed an unsigned letter:

> Mr. Editor: A few days since I met with some of the Northampton colony on their way to Minnetonka. They had previously been out to explore, and had made a selection which pleased them well. They are intelligent men and will make valuable citizens. But the manner in which they were stopped and treated in Saint Paul was anything but neighborly. They were stopped and told that the Cannon River country was the best part in the territory.

The relationship between Nichols and Nutting deteriorated. Nichols wrote, on May 23rd, "Came back and found...Nutting—waiting in a store—refuses to take any land unless he can have what Cathcart has taken." The Northampton Colony was finished by the following day. Nichols wrote, "Nutting has fully blew off and left me in limbo." Nutting took a group to Faribault for settlement. He tried to justify his course to readers in Massachusetts. "The planting of a New England Colony in Minnesota is not a failure," Levi Nutting, his brother, wrote, "although the colony...most foolishly broke up before they reached the country selected for them by their agent with so much care."

Others chose the land just south of Lake Minnetonka. They included Arba Cleaveland, George Powers of Belchertown, Henry Lyman and Joshua Moore of Easthampton plus George Galpin, Lemuel Griffin, James Ryan, William Tilton, Joshua Hillary, and James Cathcart. Nichols looked on the results with satisfaction. He wrote to his friends in Massachusetts, "The members of the colony who settled here last spring and made claims and went to work are satisfied and have done well, most of them extremely well, for the first year. Mr. A. Cleveland of Minnetonka...raised one bushel and a half of potatoes from two single ones. There is a soil in that region."

Henry Nichols accepted a call to a pastoral position in Stillwater and never lived in Chanhassen. But he visited frequently and spoke proudly of the new village in a letter to the *Minnesota Republican*.

> Was you ever at Chanhassen, Mr. Editor? Two years ago, Chanhassen was nowhere. Now, or rather last fall, it polled some fifty votes; and there is hardly a vacant claim left in the township. The settlers are far above average of new settlements, in respectability, morality, and intelligence; and rarely can a pleasanter or more desireable community be found, than that now settled in Chanhassen. Nearly in the center of the township is Lake Owassa, or Lake Hazeltine, as Surveyor Adams has named it,—a lake containing some two or three hundred acres, and surrounded by fenced farms under good cultivation.
>
> The face of the country here differs from almost every other portion of the Territory. It is not a prairie, neither is it timber, nor yet is it openings, such as we call openings in other places. There is a plenty of large heavy timber, maple, ash, oak, bass, & c., but the trees stand alone, as if a part of what had once been a heavy forest, while the rest had been taken off, without leaving a vestige behind.
>
> Sometimes not more than a dozen or twenty of these trees will be found on an acre; while again, on an acre or two they stand like a forest. They shade the ground but little, being tall with small tops, like forest trees, as indeed they are, with but little of the forest. Thus a man has the strong soil of a timber farm, without the labor of clearing off the timber.
>
> A Lyceum is well sustained, with debates every week, and the "Portfolio" published weekly. I had the pleasure of being present

last week. The gathering was at the spacious log cabin of one of the farmers, who by the way is a daguerrean artist of no mean skill, and who still pursues his business, as the sides of his room amply testified. Here the Lyceum discussed with much animation, the Land Limitation Bill, after which came the cream—the reading of the "Portfolio" by Mrs. Bingham.

The picture is the realization of Nichol's dream that he carried from Massachusetts. That of "a more desirable community" that meant good land with prosperous farms lived in by moral, literate people. A government agent concurred. He wrote, "A Post Office is established bearing the name of the township. A schoolhouse and church are now nearly completed. Every thing indicates thrift, industry, and intelligence."

The place now had a name. Mrs. Cleaveland leaves us with the first record of the town's new name. She wrote to her niece, Mariah Bardwell, on August 22, 1853 with the address of "Chan-has-san." In the margin, she added a note, asking, "You see we have named our place. It means maple-wood. Do you like it?" Although one source suggests that Nichols gave the town its name, Theodore Bost, a local farmer, gave Mrs. Cleaveland the credit. He wrote, "Strictly speaking, Chanhassen is the house belonging to the Lymans, who have a big farm. He is our postmaster. Mrs. Cleaveland gave the post office the Indian name Chanhassen and the whole township is beginning to be known by this name." They all thought it meant maple tree or sugar but it is a combination of the Dakota words for tree [chan] and hassan [berry juice]. Although there were some variations in spelling in the early years (some wrote "Chanhassan"), most used the spelling that lasted.

The name was popular at once. The *Saint Anthony Express* noted, "[Chanhassen] in our opinion is the most beautiful of all the names that have as yet been bestowed upon the fine and splendid rural districts of Minnesota." The *Minnesota Republican* newspaper noted in November, 1854: "Chanhassen is the name of a post office and settlement midway between Excelsior and Yorktown on the Minnesota. Like Excelsior and vicinity, the population are mainly from Massachusetts and are nearly all Republicans."

Bost drew a map of his neighborhood for his parents.

Some Early Families

Cleaveland

Arba and Clarissa Cleaveland were a respected couple in the new community. Clarissa was Henry Nichols' sister-in-law. Theodore Bost, a neighbor, described Cleaveland as "a tall, robust, hearty fellow. Has a good head on his shoulders. Very polite, too." His wife, Sophie Bost, wrote about Clarissa, "Mrs. Cleaveland is, I believe, the most estimable of all the women near here—pious, lively, enthusiastic, well educated, with attractive manners and a charming family of four well-behaved daughters and an excellent man for a husband…" Arba Cleaveland was elected to the territorial house of representatives in 1855 as a member of the new Republican Party. He held the post of vice-president of the State Agricultural Society as well.

Their home was on the shore of Lake Hazeltine. Mrs. Cleaveland described it to her niece back in Massachusetts. June 18, 1857:

Symbol	Meaning
+	*My Claim*
☐	*Schoolhouse & church*
☐	*Widow Maxwell*
☐	*Hobson*
☐	*Powers*
#	*Cleaveland*
##	*Fuller*
###	*Bingham*
###	*Lyman*

I live in a little log house with four windows in it; two bedrooms on the west end and a parlor, sitting room, kitching, and pantry all in one. At the east window have a beautiful view of the lake. I have made a walk down to the brook, and my flowers on either side, they are all up, and my dahlias all alive. It will look some like home to see old Mass[achusetts] plants in Minn[esota]. We have an Indian canoe on our lake. Mr. Powers goes out and gets us pond lilies: it is a pretty little sheet of water about a mile or more long.

Aspden

John Aspden was one of the oldest pioneers. He was born in England in 1808 and came to America in 1849. He brought two sons with him, Henry and James. Henry Aspden was born in England in 1837. They lived for seven years in Massachusetts where he attended college and worked at a weaving establishment. He settled in Chanhassen in 1856 when his father purchased 160 acres. He would serve as assessor and treasurer, as well as town clerk and treasurer of Chanhassen. His brother, James, was born in 1840, and served in the Civil War.

Lyman

Henry Martyn Lyman was born in Easthampton, Massachusetts, September 13, 1828. He was educated in the public schools and Williston Seminary. Henry took over the family farm after his father's death. In 1850 Mr. Lyman landed at Taylor's Falls, remaining a year after which he returned to Massachusetts. In the spring of 1853 he headed west again, landing at Saint Anthony Falls. He purchased some oxen and drove west. He built a log house of tamarack. He, too, came to stake his claim and then return to take a wife. He returned to

Mary Taylor Aspden, wife of John

Mary Wood Aspden and her brother, John Wood

Right: Henry Aspden with his cattle

Massachusetts in the fall of 1855 to marry Martha Pomeroy of Southampton in the spring of 1856.

Lyman was the first postmaster and clerk for the first election. Lyman was widely respected for his ability with agriculture and horticulture. He probably planted the first apple tree in Carver County in 1853, bringing with him six small apple trees and seeds. They all died in the winter of 1856. The *Northampton Courier*, Nov. 22, 1853 reported, "At Minnetonka, on the claim of Henry Lyman, is a meadow of fifteen acres or more of the best quality of native hay, which yields from three to five tons to the acre." Another person noted that prairie grass stood fourteen feet tall in Lyman's fields.

Powers

George Powers was born on a farm near Belchertown, Massachusetts. Like many of the Northampton Colony, he was an educated man, graduating from college with honors. His wife, Thelena White, graduated from Mount Holyoke. Powers traveled to Minnesota with the goal of claiming land, building a home, and then returning to marry. He followed his plan.

A neighbor wrote that Powers was "an excellent, handsome young man. Always happy, good Christians, very nice and pleasant." He was active in local politics, holding offices at the township and local level.

Trumble

Joel Trumble was born in 1831 in Concord, New York. While living in Illinois, he met Jemima Aldritt, followed her to Chanhassen and married her in 1857. They had ten children.

Wood

Abel Wood came to America from England as a young boy and found work in New England cotton mills. He brought his family to the Waukesha area of Wisconsin. There was malaria so they returned to Massachusetts. He began to read the series of letters that Henry Martyn Nichols sent to the *Northampton Courier* and decided to try the west again. In 1854, he and his family landed in Yorkville with a contingent that included Caspar Knott, John Aspden, and the Hobson, Lynn, and Moore families. The farmstead was a 16 x 24 foot log house with two windows, a bed made of tamarack poles, a cross leg pine board table, some stools, an iron stove and two chests of clothing from the east.

Harrison

Edward B. Harrison, a native of England, was born July 21, 1831. After duty in the English navy, Harrison settled in Chanhassen in 1855, shortly after his marriage to Hannah Richardson of England. Harrison became a prominent community leader, serving as Chair-

Abel Wood

Margaret Jackson Wood

Jemima Aldritt Trumble

Harrison farm off Galpin Road near Murray Hill South.

Mrs. James Maxwell

man of the board of supervisors for six or seven years. In 1874, he was elected to the state legislature.

Fuller

William Fuller was born in Connecticut in 1823 and came to Chanhassen with his wife, Susan, in 1854. Bost describes Fuller as a farmer and school teacher, "A well–bred gentleman, very polite." He was active in the Congregational Church. In later years, after Susan died, he married Adelle Lyman. He died in 1902.

Maxwell

Alicia Maxwell, a widow, settled near Lake Minnewashta in 1856 with two sons and two daughters. Bost describes the widow Maxwell as "a rich woman." They were "very good neighbors." Sophie Bost said, "Mrs. Maxwell is so cheerful, open, generous, and youthful. She has such a warm heart." Alicia lived until 1894. James was active in the community. He served in the Civil War and married Ellen Aspden in 1867. He died in 1897.

Aldritt

Joseph and Ann Aldritt came from England in 1854, spending two years in northern Illinois before settling in Chanhassen. Two sons, Samuel and Edwin, worked the farm.

Cheeseman

Rufus Cheeseman, a lay Methodist minister, worked a farm and apparently did stone masonry. He was born in New York in 1822.

Bennett

They lived in Excelsior then purchased land in Chanhassen in 1859. Isaac and Ruth Bennett had four sons and three daughters.

Leach

Alonzo Leach was born in Caledonia County, Vermont in 1835. At ten, he moved to Chickopee, Massachusetts—the same region as the Northampton Colony. Leach came to Minnesota in 1857 on the west bank of Lake Minnewashta. He married Rhoda Aldritt in 1859 and they had eight children. Mr. Leach served on the school board and served in the Civil War.

Judd

Burritt and William Judd, two brothers from Connecticut, settled in Section 11 and 12. Although they were New Englanders, they were Episcopalians. Burritt was a talented architect and builder. His family had spent the previous year in Little Rock, Arkansas but came north to live near Clara's father, D.H. Hull. When Chaska attempted to grab the county seat, they hired Judd to construct several county buildings. He built three churches in Minneapolis and gained a national reputation. The Judds served as lay missionaries for the Episcopal Church and Burritt became the second person ordained in Minnesota. He was "an excellent and zealous churchman," said Rev. Josiah Chamberlain. William Judd listed his occupation as "daugerian"—a photographer. It was undoubtably an exotic profession in rural Minnesota.

In late 1858 Burritt Judd decided to move again. His wife, Clara, was suffering from poor health. He took a post at the University of

Alonzo and Rhoda (Aldritt) Leach

Front row: James Arthur Wilson, Ruth Bennett and Isaac Bennett holding Olive Wilson. Back row: Miriam Bennett Wilson, Willis Wilson, and Hattie Wilson. Photograph taken 1909.

CHANHASSEN: A CENTENNIAL HISTORY 31

*Bost Family, 1874.
Left to right: Theodore, Alice
(on lap), Julie, Alphonse,
Theodore Jr., Sophie*

*Right: Bost drew a map of his
farm. The house is still
standing on the property of the
Minnesota Arboretum.*

1. Marsh.
2. Old house.
3. Garden.
4. Well.
5. Stable.
6–9. Magnificent field.
10. Present house.
11. Chicken coop.
12. Barnyard.
13–14. Field cleared.
15. Small woodlot.
16. Small meadow.
17. Maxwells' house.
18. Bee tree.

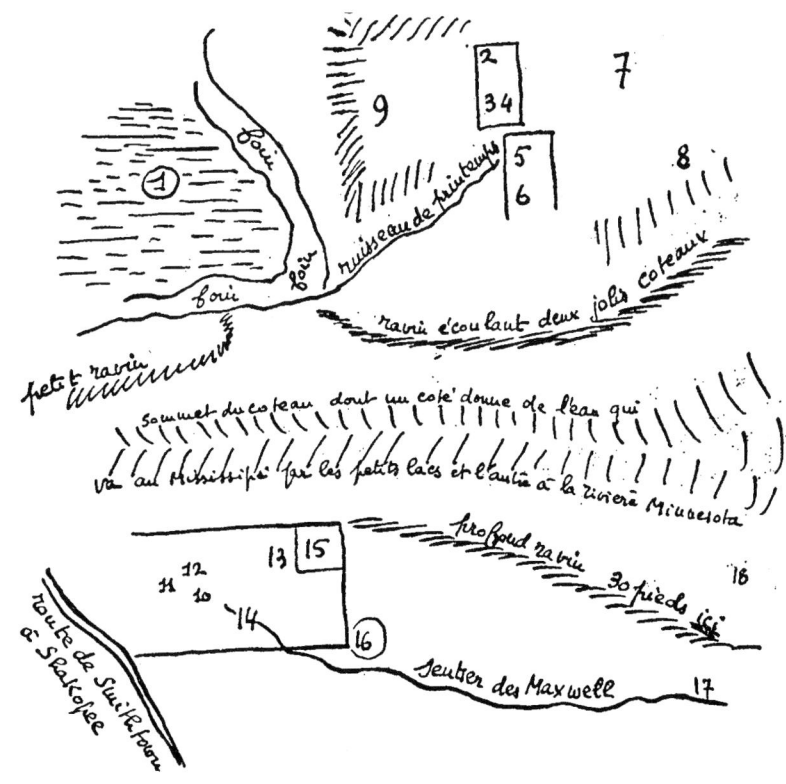

the South in Sewanee, Tennessee and apparently supervised the construction of the first campus buildings. They left a permament reminder of their stay—they named Lake Lucy after their five-year-old daughter. Lake Ann was named after William's wife.

Theodore Bost

Theodore Bost came from Switzerland and settled in Chanhassen in November, 1855. He was a regular correspondent throughout his life and his many letters provide us with the most detailed look at life in early Chanhassen. After landing at Chaska, he began walking through the woods, checking possible claims. "The claim I've just bought was occupied by a railroad engineer who thought he'd like farming but got tired of it....Another good point of this claim is that the people round about are English or American, either Christians or at least churchgoers, ready to lend a hand to their neighbors and to protect one another's claims."

Bost was a strongly opininated man from a strict Protestant family. Along with Cleaveland, Lyman and Powers, he immersed himself in Republican politics.

Life on the Frontier

The pioneers remembered the early years of Chanhassen as hard yet Edwin Aldritt wrote, "Those were happy days. We were all good friends and every man helped his neighbor. Frequently we would drive ten or twenty miles to visit some family and if a new homesteader came to the country we would all help him build his cabin." There were no tradespeople, no shopkeepers. Everyone farmed the land.

Theodore Bost described his home to his parents in Switzerland:

> I moved into the old log cabin, which is eight feet square, four feet high at the north end, and seven feet high at the south end. Before moving in I took some earth from the cellar, mixed water with it, and then threw it with all four fingers and my thumb between the logs of the cabin walls so that I am cozy and warm and in the morning when I wash I have hardly any ice in my room instead of seeing my drinking water turned to ice.
>
> The cabin is now my bedroom, living room, dining room, pantry, etc. and if I stay near the door I can spin around three times in a row. . .without knocking anything over. Seated on my empty nail keg, I can do everything I need to do without getting up; I tend my fire by leaning over to my right, where I also keep my kettle; then I keep my lamp, a tin can, a cup, etc.; then still perched on my keg, by leaning over backward I land on my bed which serves me as a backrest.

The farms provided most of the necessities of life. There were few cash transactions. Benedict Schmid kept a careful accounting. For example, his total expenses for the year 1862 were:

Jan. 8	Shoe soles	.35
Jan 12	Pants	.85
Jan 17	Postage and thread	.25
Feb 7	Shirt material and spoon	2.65
Feb 8	Income Tax	3.85
Feb 11	Wash kettle, copper wash boiler	.75
Feb 15	Salt, shoes for child, pants	4.20
Feb 22	paper and ink	.15
Mar 8	Starch and braid	.40
May	School tax	.40
May 8	Hat and other small items	4.40
	Blacksmith	1.00
May 20	Smith's plow and trivet ax	3.75
June 1	Shoes and material	3.76
June 15	Harrow teeth, fork and other items	5.60
June 29	Agricultural paper	1.80
July 11	Poll tax	1.00
Aug 16	Calf	1.25
Aug 24	Caliper, schnapps, strap, items	4.10
Sept 3	Cotton material	9.70
Sept 21	Boots, pants material, underpants	7.15
	Fixing plow	.88
Oct.	Pig, bowls, string, glass	1.80
Oct 20	Wagon	60.00
	Coat, underwear, pants, rope	11.30
	Threshing, nails	13.00
Nov. 8	Shoes, shirts	7.25
Nov. 15	Linen for pants	1.33
Nov 23	Linen and small items	1.90
	Geese	1.00
Dec 20	Midwife	2.00

For cash, he sold wheat, corn, rye, potatoes, green beans, and two and a half pigs.

The farmers found that the land was good. Nature provided the direst threats. Clarissa Cleaveland wrote about one danger.

> The prairie fires...have been raging all the month. Some nights, when there is no moon, the whole heavens are illumined and it looks like one mighty conflagration. Other nights, when the fire is near I can see to pick up a pin anywhere, but it does not

Susan Hazeltine started the first school in Carver County in 1855. The schoolhouse was located along a lake that bears her name.

frighten me at all, for I know it is harming no one, or at least it will not, if they take the precaution they should to burn around everything they have. I have heard of but one being burned out near us and that was a German 3 miles west of us. The country is so destitute of mountains or large hills that we can see the reflections of fires that are miles & miles, distant.

The threat of prairie fire was real. A few years later, the Bosts lost their stable, fence, and hay. Bost explained, "There was a man about two miles from here who set fire to a pile of weeds in his garden and then was unable to prevent the fire from spreading into the woods and marshes. Several of our neighbors had their fences burned up. If the unlucky wretch who did such a good job of burning his weeds had a penny to his name, he would lose it all in lawsuits but he is a poor Methodist minister." Rufus Cheeseman, the minister, remained in poverty for years to come.

Since the New Englanders were all educated, the establishment of a school was very important. The Cleavelands brought Susan Hazeltine to their home in 1855. She began the first school in Carver County and made such an impression that two lakes were named after her. Two years later, the county established official school districts.

The social life of the community centered around the new schoolhouse. Theodore Bost wrote, "Our surroundings are excellent; a schoolhouse and church are half a mile away; there are social gatherings in winter where men and youths hold discussions on all sorts of subjects….There aren't many places where he would find ways to spend money, unless he were to go to Shakopee, and I'm sure he wouldn't want to associate with that crowd of young rascals."

Mary Wood Aspden remembered the spelling bees, debates, and lyceum meetings at the District Twelve Schoolhouse. She wrote a poem on mosquitoes:

> And if they ever come again
> To torment and to vex us.
> I hope a good strong wind shall come
> And blow them all to Texas.

Love and Marriage

Life on the Minnesota frontier was a challenge. Most of the Northampton Colony brought families with them. Others came alone with hopes of bringing their wives later. A few were bachelors who needed to secure a farm before they married.

Theodore Bost worked alone on his farm for several years before he turned to the pursuit of matrimony. Obviously, there were few available women in the township and Bost evaluated each one with a careful eye. "Fanny Maxwell is the only girl hereabouts that I could love, but—always supposing she were willing to marry me—I hesitate to tie myself in that way to such a family," he wrote his parents. "I don't like to put my reasons on paper in detail; but the word "debauche" could be used in a general sort of way....It is really disgusting to see a lady who wants to pass for a Christian behaving this way."

He wrote to his parents for advice and they suggested that Sophie Bonjour, a young girl living in Switzerland, was interested. He remembered Sophie, although Theodore at first thought that her older sister, Marie, was the intended. Still, he courted her for two and a half years. He assured his parents, "Are they afraid that I am too isolated? But, just as I am now, I have two neighbors within a half a mile...If Sophie and I should want to, we could build a house between these two neighbors, the Maxwells and the Moores."

Sophie finally consented and traveled to Minnesota. Bost met her in Saint Paul and they were married the following day. They remained together until Theodore's death in 1919 in San Dimas, California.

Benedict Schmid and Rosina Auer

Benedict Schmid returned to Minnesota in 1858 and built a home northwest of Lake Minnewashta. Once the first growing season was completed, Benedict's mind turned to his next acquisition— a wife to help with the chores. His quest was not easy but he was single-minded in his pursuit.

On December 13, 1858, he recorded his first attempt. He wrote,

> I went to Chaska to see what Louisa is made from. I asked her to marry me but she declined, she said she is too young to get married. That answer is ten cents worth. Well that's how it is. I am not going to shoot a bullet through my head or drown myself. The water is frozen over anyway. It would be too much work to chop a hole in the ice and besides, the water would be much too cold for such love play. So I live like nothing happened…I can't find a reason for her actions unless it was because it was a cold day and I presume it formed an ice circle around her heart and my simple phrases could not melt it. That's why the love bounced back like a bullet from a rock. It is probably the best to wait till I come to my senses. Well this is how my first courting ended. Experience makes a guy wise.

This "wiser" Schmid tried again just two weeks later. On Christmas Day, he wrote, "I went to Fischer and asked his daughter for her hand. She said she didn't know so I asked Fischer. He said he couldn't give her a dowry. He hasn't got anything to give. Now I got kicked a second time. I went and asked Shultz to ask Matthias if he would like to write a letter for me to his sister. He said she wants to get married if she can get a decent fellow."

He recovered sufficiently to try again the following day—his third proposal in two weeks! He wrote, "I went to Saint Paul to talk to Rosina Auer. I had never seen her before. She looked pretty small but well built, a round face with a button nose. I handed her the letter and asked her about getting married. She didn't want to come right out and say what she thinks, she was surprised."

Finally discouraged, Schmid threw himself into farm work. Finally, in the spring, he found his wife.

> May 17, 1859: Rosina promised to marry me if we have the pastor take care of the legalization.
> May 27, 1859: I married Rosina Auer. Patience and Gentleness My Motto Be. Here is where the 2nd part of my life begins.
> May 28, 1859: I made a pig barn and helped Matthias put up some beans.

Benedict Schmid was settled now that he had the hand of Rosina. He returned to work the land and begin building a community.

Chanhassen Township

As the population grew, the new residents organized a local government, acting under the requirements of a territory. Chanhassen created a precinct in 1854, becoming the first township in Carver County. Carver was not declared an organized county until March 3, 1855 after an act of the territorial legislature established twenty–four new counties. The first general election was held at the home of Arba Cleaveland in the fall of 1855. Several Chanhassen men won posts, including Burritt S. Judd, County Board; Joseph Kessler, Coroner; and George Powers, Assessor for District One.

The men gathered in the schoolhouse on May 11th, 1858 to organize the township government. They elected Timothy McArty, a farmer who lived north of Henry Lyman, as moderator of the meeting. The first order of business was the official acceptance of "Chanhassen" as the name of their community. F. A. Renz, the wealthiest man in the township, was elected chairman. Other officers included Timothy McArty and Stillman Read, supervisors; George Powers, clerk; D. H. Hull, assessor; Joseph Vogel, collector; Joseph Kessler and William S. Judd, justices of the peace; Ferdinand Wisrching, overseer of the poor; John Ess and William Trowbridge, constables; Jesse J. Sucklin, George Galpin, William Sarver, and Martin M. Schneider, overseers of the four road districts. The winners balanced the Germans and the Yankees in an even manner.

Township business focused on the local roads. When the township formed, the only two roads were the state road from Fort Snelling to Fort Ridgely and the county road between Chaska and Excelsior. Neighbors would petition the annual town meeting for tax funds for roads. The whole was divided into districts. At every town meeting, district superintendents were chosen. Men sought the position because they could earn extra income from the road work in their districts.

To pay for the road work, the township had to collect taxes. This caused an immediate problem when most residents read the first assessment. The Supervisors called a special town meeting on August 5th after they heard a tide of complaints. After examining the assessment records, they found them so imperfect that the supervisors requested the assessor, D.H. Hull, to reassess the town. Hull, probably the second wealthiest man in the township, apparently approached his task in a haphazard manner. It is not clear from the records whether the objections resulted from special favors or simple ineptitude. The supervisors ordered George Powers, the town clerk, "to procure a supply of black assessment books and deliver them together with the old assessment roll and request for a reassessment to the assessor." Hull abruptly refused to change his records, leading several townspeople to petition for a special town meeting. At that September meeting, Knight Whipple was appointed to replace Hull, who resigned in the face of united opposition.

Churches

The center of the community, as it was in the New England society, was the church. A church, referred to by Bost as a "Union" church, was officially formed on July 17, 1853 under the direction of the Reverend Charles Galpin. Tradition says that the first services were held under maple trees on Henry Lyman's farm, once every two weeks. The minister would preach in Excelsior in the morning and travel to Chanhassen for an afternoon service. Later, the church met in a schoolhouse. James Cathcart wrote to his friends in Massachusetts, "We have a little church formed and as one of our number is a Congregational Minister, we have regular preaching on the Sabbath. My nearest neighbors are all Eastern men and of the right stamp—enterprising, intelligent, and most of them pious." Eventually, all the services were held at the First Independant Church of Chanhassen and Excelsior. It later became the Excelsior Congregational Church in 1906.

The Judds tried to establish an Episcopal church in the township. In 1854 Burritt was licensed as a lay reader and conducted services in his home. Chamberlain visited the Judd home, reporting to a superior, "A year ago, I believe there was not a single settler there, and even now, my way thither for the last eight or nine miles of it is through unbroken solitude; and yet, twenty-five persons, at least, I think, were assembled for service at my last visit. The sects have as yet no hold there."

In 1855, the Chanhassen church was organized and a church was built. Saint John's in Chanhassen was a twenty by forty foot frame structure with a small chancel. The cornerstone was set on May 18, 1855. After Chamberlain and Judd left and C.W. Rees, a prominent church member, moved to Eden

Saint John's Episcopal Church was built in Chanhassen but moved to Eden Prairie in 1866.

Minnewashta Union Congregational Church, circa 1920

Prairie, the congregation faltered. In 1866 the building was moved to a site on Pioneer Trail in Eden Prairie. With the demise of Saint John's, the township went without a Protestant church until the 1970s.

Farewell to the Nichols and Cleavelands

Nichols served for several years as pastor of the Stillwater Presbyterian Church. He became well known for his fiery speeches against slavery and for temperance. "I come to you tonight as an agitator," he began a powerful abolitionist lecture. His interest in improving the moral life of the state never diminished. In 1859 he accepted a call as pastor of Plymouth Congregational Church in Minneapolis. On March 26, 1860, Parker M. Edgerly, a twenty-three year old clerk at a local hotel, died from delerium tremens with Henry and Nancy Nichols at his bedside. Deeply moved, Nichols preached the most powerful sermon of his life on the next Sunday. The house was packed. He told the young men to "dash away" the beer glass before it was too late. He called on the mothers to close up the bars. On Monday morning, impromptu "Dashaway Clubs" were formed and a committee of women began calling on every saloon in the city. Weary of the emotional pitch, Nichols visited his sister's home in Chanhassen for a few days. On his return, he learned that Plymouth Church had been burned to the ground. The *Falls Evening News* reported that the fire had been set on both sides of the church. The *State Atlas* declared, "The liquor traffic in this community having written its history in letters of blood, it was no more

William Sarver house was completed in 1859. It is still standing on Hwy. 41 just south of Hwy. 5.

than proper...that it be read by the light of burning churches."

Nancy Nichols wrote in her diary that friends "would not let him walk the streets alone. There is a watch set over the house last night to prevent its being fired, as there is such a feeling against Mr. N by the saloon keepers." He began carrying a revolver.

But the congregation chose to rebuild. In late June, Nichols wrote in his diary, "prospect brightens for a new church." It was his last entry. On July 5th, he joined Arba Cleaveland for a picnic at Lake Calhoun. The two oldest Cleaveland girls and young Henry Jr. went swimming and stepped over a steep slope into deep water. The two fathers dashed into the water and sank beneath its surface. At the last minute, Nancy reached out her hand to her husband, the hand that had held her on the S.B. Dr. Franklin seven years earlier. She called back to her sister to head for shore then sank clutching her husband. The next afternoon, six coffins were placed on the lawn of the Nichols home. Thousands attended his funeral. It was the great tragedy of the era before the Civil War, the moment when a city stops and searches its soul.

Theodore Bost, who thought so highly of the Cleavelands, wrote, "So there was Mrs. Cleaveland in a strange town, alone in a hotel with the dead bodies of her husband, her oldest girls, her sister, her brother-in-law, and her nephew, with nobody to console her except for two little girls of seven and four years of age."

Life went on, even after a tragedy. Sophie and Theodore tried to watch over the widow and offered to take her in for the winter. They wrote to his parents on September 22, 1860,

> Mrs. Cleaveland is not going to spend the winter with us...She has decided to go back East to her family. So now the most delightful family around here has been lost and destroyed. Mrs. Cleaveland has been selling her furniture and so on, we have seized the opportunity to buy for not much money a lot of things we should otherwise have had to buy a few at a time—a lovely, solid dresser, a good sofa, a kitchen stove, a small worktable, and a number of other things.

A year later, several of the neighbors met at the schoolhouse to organize the Chanhassen Cemetery Association. The initial members were Hiram Eldridge, John Murray, Theodore Bost, Henry Lyman, William Sarver, George Powers, and Harlow Langdon. They selected a piece of land owned by John Murray, probably selected because it held the grave of Nirum Abbott. After they divided the lots, they reserved one for Clarissa Cleaveland. Her husband and daughters are buried there. It was the final step for the Northampton colonists. Chanhassen was now their final resting place.

Nancy Sikes Nichols was the sister of Clarissa Cleaveland and the wife of Reverend Henry Nichols. She died alongside her husband in a drowning at Lake Calhoun.

Chanhassen Pioneer Cemetery on Galpin Boulevard. In 1985 the private cemetery association transferred ownership to the city.

Alice Bost, daughter of Theodore and Sophie, died in 1865. Bost was a founding member of the Chanhassen Cemetery Association.

Chapter Three
Divisions

CHANHASSEN FACED A SERIES OF CRISES IN THE 1860s that threatened the social fabric of the new community. The township was constantly changing as new immigrants settled in the county. Most of the newcomers were very different from the Yankees.

More German Catholics settled in the northeast corner of Chanhassen Township. John L. Geiser's story seems typical. He came from Wortenburg, Germany. Traveling alone, Geiser landed in Baltimore and came across country in 1834 to Salem, Ohio. He married Mary Weimer and they settled, with Mary's parents, in Noble County, Indiana in 1836. They stayed there for thirty years. During the Civil War, Geiser and four children moved to Chanhassen on a farm north of Lake Susan. He quickly rose to prominence among his countrymen.

Dutch Catholics settled in the 1850s in Chanhassen and Benton Townships. It was the largest single concentration of immigrants from Holland in the state. The *Minnesota Pioneer* of December 1, 1863 reported, "A Dutch Colony of twenty-five families has settled within ten miles of Minnetonka Lake at a place called Bavaria Lake. They are direct from the 'Faderland' and are industrious, temperate, and several of them quite wealthy." Most came from the Limburg province in Holland. This district was culturally closer to their Belgian and German neighbors than the Protestants Dutch to the north.

One scholar investigated their social background. Dr. Schrynemakers argued that these immigrants were drawn by the magnet of open land rather than being pushed by social and economic conditions at home. He wrote, "I found that most of them were modest farmers, some were well-to-do, while only a small number were poor....The great majority of those immigrants left in order to find more and better opportunities in America. The prospect of owning far more land than in the old country seems to have a special appeal for them." Their names included the Notermanns, Schutrops, Heutmakers, Timmers, and Van Slouns. Theodore and Maria Notermann, for example, came in 1863 and settled near Lake Bavaria. His son, Arnold, was sixteen at the time and worked on the farm. Like many of the settlers, the Noterman's social life centered around Victoria, a hamlet to the north of Lake Bavaria.

Maria Reijs Notermann, wife of Theodore, was born in Switzerland in 1853. Three granddaughters married three Schneider boys.

Theodore Bost noticed the changes. He wrote, "This year the price of land doubled on account of an influx of Dutch settlers, but there's hardly anybody except the Germans who can sell to them because the latter tell the newcomers to have nothing to do with the Americans." His new neighbors concerned him. "If another pack of Germans should move in, it's not impossible that I might sell out, not wanting to be stuck in the middle of such a bunch of ignorant Democrats." Sophie complained that the Germans—"all ignorant lower-class people—are becoming more numerous around us." Other immigrants came from Luxemborg. They included the Klingelhutzes, Paulys and Kleins.

The Dakota War

The land had been open for settlement for a decade. Although, technically, the Native American population had all been removed to reservations, they continued to have a presence around Chanhassen.

Descriptions of Indian life have been filtered through the eyes of a different culture. Family tradition says that Veronica Vogel would often give bread to Indian visitors. The Bennett family states the same story about their mother. Even older residents recall similar tales in their lifetimes. Henry Dimler remembers some coming to Carver Beach every year to dig ginseng roots and gather lotus leaves. "We were scared of the Indians," he said.

The early pioneers had seen the possible violence first hand. When the Ojibway moved into northern Minnesota after white settlement forced them west of their traditional homes, they pushed the Dakota

Theresa (Diethelm) and Arnold Notermann. Notermann was among the Chanhassen settlers from the Limburg area of Holland. Although he farmed in Chanhassen, many people associate him with Victoria where he ran a store.

Site of battle between the Dakota and the Ojibway in 1858. Photograph taken in the 1920s.

to lands further south. Chanhassen stood along the imaginary border. The dispute led to a fierce battle near Rice Lake on May 27, 1858. Hundreds of Shakopee residents stood on the bluffs to watch the combat. Mary Wood remembered several Dakota men riding through the streets of that town, preparing for the battle. At night, she visited their camp and watched their ceremonies.

> The Chippewa's scalp was hung on a pole in the center of a circle of Indians. As the bright flames of a campfire cast weird shadows of the dancing Indians upon the trees and tents about them, the braves shuffled their feet in an odd fashion as they moved about the scalp, shouting "Hey-yah! Hey-yah! Hey-yah!" This dancing was continued nightly until...the battle between the two tribes.

The Ojibway (Chippewa) used routes through Chanhassen and they retreated through town to the relative safety of Lake Minnetonka.

The simmering tensions between the Dakota and the European population erupted in the summer of 1862. Chanhassen was distant from the bloodshed but rumors swept across the fields like a prairie wildfire.

Theodore Bost scribbled a quick letter to his parents, telling them in early August, "Early this morning I learned that the Yankton [Indians] and the Sioux were five miles from our home, killing and burning everyone and everything, and I must go to Chaska to join the forces being organized there...I consider the whole thing another humbug...The nearest they are known to be is eighty miles away. You [would] have no idea what a commotion there was. Everybody stopped harvesting crops, three out of four [had left] with their families, bagage, animals, etc.; many had left their wheat stacks half-finished outdoors." The Bosts had "more occasions for enjoying a good laugh at the expense of those who were most eagerly panicked."

Sophie Bost was not as cavalier. She wrote, "I dreamed night before last that my children were butchered before my eyes." Her neighbors were even more fearful. Sophie wrote, "Mrs. Cheeseman came in with her four children whom she hadn't waited to wash and comb. On the way home, I looked in at the Sarvers' and found the wife pale with fear and the children weeping, the father molding bullets for his musket and about to leave at top speed for Chaska, which is the assembly point. Great numbers of neighbors piled what they could onto their wagons and departed; others were standing watch, ready to leave at a

Members of the Dakotas remained a part of Chanhassen life despite government efforts to remove them. This photograph was taken in the early 1900s. Many older people remember annual trips by the Shakopee settlement to Lotus (Long) Lake.

moment's notice. We were all at the point of bundling up a few valuables and leaving for Fort Snelling where the garrison is."

Mary Wood Aspden remembered that her father had gone out to cut hay with a scythe and Mrs. Wood was visiting a neighbor. The two children set out to find their father but couldn't find him. When they returned, they found the door open. Fearing the worst, they looked in to see their father. "If the Indians want to destroy my property," he said, "he might as well be killed by them." She said that some Excelsior people headed for Big Island in Lake Minnetonka while others scurried to Fort Snelling. Ruth Bennett relates a similar family escape to Big Island.

The Civil War

When the Civil War began, there was no surge of patriotic fervor that swept other towns in Minnesota. Theodore Bost, a Republican, supported the war. In May 1861, he wrote, "Have I ever told you I'm the only person hereabouts who wants to see slavery abolished? The Republicans want only its non-extension but I want abolition which is a different matter." In the end, fifty men from Chanhassen served in the Civil War. Most of these soldiers went reluctantly, though, called up in the drafts of 1864.

It was not easy. William Maxwell enlisted and served in the Second Minnesota Infantry. Sophie Bost wrote, "Some of our neighbors have suffered very badly—among others, Mrs. Maxwell who, not having any able–bodied men at home, can't have a snug, warm house. We've found her all dressed up as though she were going to pay visits, wearing a hood and covered with shawls, sitting hunched over the stove. Her health has been ruined. The poor woman! The only son she has left at home is a drunkard." George Powers' brother-in-law was captured while in the army and held in a prison camp. Theodore Bost noted on January 24, 1865 that, "Mrs. Powers' brother has just been liberated by an exchange of prisoners from the mud hut where he was kept, and he was in such wasted condition when he arrived in the North that he didn't even have enough ambition to write anyone for six weeks."

Edwin Aldritt, Civil War veteran, in his GAR uniform.

Not everyone came home. Israel Trumble enlisted in February 1864. He was assigned to a post in Rolla, Missouri with the Ninth Minnesota Regiment and died from an illness. His widow, Jane, tried to contact the military but apparently never learned more about his death. He left three children. Alexander Livingston died at the battle of Antietam.

"I Never Saw Such Shooting"

Edwin Aldritt was twenty-one when the war began. He enlisted in the fall of 1861 and had a distinguished career in the Army as a member of the Second United States Sharpshooters in March 1862. By the time the war ended, Aldritt saw action in forty-two battles including Fredericksburg, Chancellorsville, Antietam, Gettysburg, the second battle of Bull Run, Malvern Hill, Wilderness, and Petersburg.

His unit played an important role in the battle of Gettysburg. He later remembered,

> The day before the Gettysburg battle I was detailed by my colonel to go out alone several times from our line of march and climb a high hill that commanded sight of the valleys leading to Gettysburg. The Union troops then were converging on Gettysburg. I reached the hill—it was almost a mountain—and working my way up the slope when I spotted a Rebel sharpshooter standing behind a tree not twenty feet away. He was watching our army. We saw each other at the same time and we both fired at the same time. His bullet scorched my ribs—a half an inch deeper and his would have brought me down. My bullet grazed his nose and cut a slash about his cheek. We both started to reload but as he had an old muzzle-loading squirrel rifle and I had a new breech-loader, I had my cartridge in firsthand. I yelled to him to throw up his hands.
>
> "You've got the drop on me, Yank," he said, and threw down his gun. He seemed greatly bothered because I got the drop on him and finally asked me what state I was from. I told him Minnesota. "Oh," he said, "you're one of them Minnesoty woodsmen. No wonder you got the drop on me."

John Livingston was a sharp shooter in the Civil War.

On the second day of the battle, Aldritt was assigned to the Union left. General Daniel Sickles had moved his Corps into a peach orchard, leaving gaps in the main federal line. An Alabama brigade began its attack in the late afternoon and threatened to punch through the hole left by Sickle's unauthorized advance. Seeing the danger, the Sharpshooters were told to take up positions and delay the Confederates until reinforcements could come up.

Aldritt tells his story:

Right: Edwin Aldritt and Anna Mann Aldritt. Below: The Aldritt home on Red Cedar Point on Lake Minnewashta

Pettyjohn and I each took one side of the road. He could scout like an Indian and so could I. I never moved more than ten feet without scanning the ground and I also was laying out a safe route for my retreat. Soon I came to a clearing where a woman was sitting on the porch of a house. As I stood reconnoitering, I saw a boy come running out of the opposite side of the clearing.

"Mama, mama!" He called to the woman, "the woods back there is filled with men in gray. It's just thick with them and they have cannon, too."

"You're mistaken," she said, "for the Union troops went here yesterday and there aren't any rebels around."

"Yes there are," he said. I didn't wait for any more. I ran across the clearing, not paying any attention to the woman and the boy, and behind the house I saw a stone smokehouse like those Pennsylvanians used in which to cure meat. It was on top of a small hill at the base of which, not fifty yards away, was the Confederate skirmish line. A little to my left, towards the Emmittsburg Pike, was the main body of the infantry and in front of the infantry was a group of mounted officers looking at a map.

Just as I was looking I heard a rifle report and the man holding the map tumbled from his horse. It was Pettyjohn who had fired. Instantly, I blazed away at the group of officers and turned to run for my life. As I started to run the Confederate skirmishers fired a volley at the smokehouse. I could hear the lead smash up against it. I had fifty yards start and by the time those first Johnnies got to the top of the hill I was across the clearing hiding behind some big rocks. I fired several shots at them before they could find me and then I dusted for our lines. The boys were amply warned by the shooting and we beat back the first Confederate attack.

We sharpshooters were behind a stone wall and we made a quick work of the skirmishers. They brought up a regiment but had no chance. They had come across a clearing of about 200 yards and we shot them to pieces. Their loss was terrible and they didn't get half way before they broke and ran back for the woods.

Our colonel told me to scout across the clearing to learn if they had retired or were bringing up reinforcements. I started and suddenly came across a wounded Confederate major. I gave him a swig out of my canteen and then he asked: "What regiment is that behind the wall?" I told him we were the Second United States Sharpshooters. "My God," he said again, "I never saw such shooting." Col. W.S. Oats of the 15th Alabama said after the war, "I think I would have captured Round Top and won the battle of Gettysburg."

Pickett's Charge

On July 3rd, the Confederates gathered their troops for an assault on the Union center—Pickett's Charge. The attack would come over an open field with clear visibility for almost one mile. It was an ideal mission for the Sharpshooters. Even the slightest delay in the Rebel advance exposed their soldiers to withering cannon fire. Aldritt remembered,

We lay there a couple of hours, listening to the most terrible artillery fire I ever heard before or since. Shells went screaming overhead and the ground shook as if by earthquake. Finally the Union batteries slackened their fire…and a few minutes later we could see the long gray columns of the Confederates burst from the woods on Seminary Hill and come down the slopes. There seemed to be a million of them.

A young staff officer galloped out to where we lay about 500 yards in advance of the Union lines. "Hold 'em, sharpshooters," he yelled. "Gibbons is bringing up reinforcement but there is a weak spot in the line and you've got to hold them!" Then he galloped off.

"How can a few sharpshooters hold that mass," I thought to myself, but I didn't have long to think, for soon they were within range and we were firing into the thick of them. I was so busy that the first thing I noticed was that the left of the enemy had swung past me toward the Union line and I didn't have a chance in the world to get back. The boys on the left and the right had most of them worked back safely but I had been lying behind a big rock firing and hadn't seen my danger. I decided that my only chance lay in pretending to be dead. I rolled between two logs, flat on my face, and a few seconds later the Johnnies came surging over me like a big wave and went on for the Union line.

After the charge failed, "the Johnnies went back faster than they came and the minute the last man had passed I started for the Union lines. I was a pretty good runner and I broke all my records that day. I expected to be killed and pretended to be dead twice and it took some time to make myself believe that I really wasn't.

During the siege of Petersburg, Aldritt learned about the value of a long range rifle in trench warfare. For months, the opposing armies sat opposite each other, often with shooting distance of the enemy. When a southern sniper shot thirteen gunners at an artillery position, the captain of the federal battery asked for the help of the sharpshooters. Aldritt said,

I had a special rifle with a telescopic sight. I took cover behind some sand bags and started to spy out the Confederate front. I commenced to cover the land, a foot at a time, and with my telescopic attachment I studied everything. I was there all morning. Finally, early in the afternoon, I saw a gate post about sixteen inches square which had a beveled hole through it about four inches square for the latch. 'Ha, that looks like a good place for a sharpshooter,' I thought to myself. 'I'll watch that post.' Watch it I did for five or ten minutes and finally I saw some dirt move down at the bottom of the post. Then I saw the muzzle of a rifle barrel come through the hole. He fired and disappeared in a second, but I thought, "I'll get you next time old boy."

I called the captain of the batteries over. "Let's see him," he asked. I told him to look through the telescope. "Why he's sticking his gun through that hole now," the captain said. "Shoot him," I replied. "I can't hit," the captain answered. "If you can see him through the sight of the gun, it is aimed all right," I answered and the captain fired. He drilled that Johnnie right through the forehead and the battery didn't lose any more men.

Aldritt came home to live a quiet life and became active in the Grand Army of the Republic.

Clara Judd

The war touched many lives, sometimes in ways that the people of Chanhassen could scarcely imagine. Burritt and Clara Judd moved away from Chanhassen in the fall of 1859, heading south. In 1861, Burritt was looking at some statuary in Nashville when he accidently stepped off the platform. He died four weeks later, leaving a widow with seven children and no means of financial support. Even worse, she lived in a country at war.

In the summer of 1862, Clara Judd returned to Chanhassen to mortgage the family farm. Many of the neighbors apparently questioned Mrs. Judd on her desire to return south. Rumors spread that she was a spy. A few months later, Clara was arrested. The story reads like a novel. In the fall of 1862, Union and Confederate forces struggled for control of Kentucky and Tennessee. The South made a concerted drive north. General John Morgan, a flamboyant cavalry officer, took troops north into Kentucky. Fear gripped the federal commanders. Nashville, the first captured major city of the Confederacy, became a hot house for spies, counter-spies, and informants.

Clara Judd made numerous trips between the lines—scarcely unusual since she had lived in Tennessee. On the sixteenth of December, while walking along the road leading between Murfreesboro and Nashville, she was offered a ride by a gentleman named Forsythe. During the ride, the two began to talk. "We soon seemed like old acquaintants," she later said. "He told me he was from Connecticut. My husband and parents were from there." At the Union lines, they came across a small group of southerners who came for meetings under a flag of truce. Mr. Forsythe held a pass and was permitted to cross the lines. Mrs. Judd was not. Forsythe later testified that he overheard one of the rebels whisper to her, "If they won't let you in, you can go across country, about four miles to my father's, and there they will run you through the lines anyhow." He grew suspicious. But they permitted Clara to cross.

Clara Judd was arrested as a Confederate spy during the Civil War and held at Alton prison near St. Louis.

Once in Nashville, he continued to see Mrs. Judd. When he was sick, she came to nurse him. A contemporary newspaper account claimed, "In addition to her confidence, he seemed now to have gained her affections. She devoted herself to him as only women do to those whom they love—anticipating his slightest wishes and providing for his every want in the most warm-hearted and loving manner."

Forsythe accompanied her on a train trip into Kentucky. Tipped to her presence, Federal troops stopped the train and arrested Mrs. Judd and Forsythe. In her trunk, they found medical supplies and a knitting machine. There was also a Bible. In the front, she had written Forsythe's name. They were brought to Nashville and she was placed under guard at a hotel. Trying to trick her, her captors told her that Forsythe would be hung in the morning. The newspaper reported that she confessed that the whole arrangement was hers alone in order to save his life. To her surprise, he was a double–spy.

Was Clara Judd a spy or a victim? Was she a jilted lover, as the newspapers said? Her case never came to trial. She was taken to the federal prison in Alton, Illinois and detained for several months. Lacking proper facilities for women prisoners, Judd was released. She issued a statement denying any guilt, stating that she had been duped. "He has sworn falsely and misrepresented other things then said jocosely."

When she returned to Minnesota, the press decided her guilt. The Chaska paper said, "She passes under the assumed name of Mrs. Jennie Smith." She was an embittered woman. This "wayward sister," as the *Chaska Weekly Herald* called her, spoke "within an air of boldness and vindictiveness unbecoming her sex. She denounces the government and all its adherents, and boasts that if she was engaged in treasonable acts, her fertile brain furnishes ample means of secrecy and escape."

The Draft

Beginning in the summer of 1863, the north began to fill its ranks with draftees. In the three draft calls of 1864, the War Department gave districts a quota based on the required number of soldiers and adjusted for the number already enlisted within the district.

Engelbert Schneider's wife explained the problems to the family in Germany.

> Each township has to furnish so many men. Now some men were able to buy their way out. Some townships furnished all its men and some haven't furnished any. For instance, our township hasn't furnished any and needs seventy men, so now my husband got drafted. If the township would have come up with the money and bought its men, it would have averaged for the most about $30 per man. Now there were many Americans and nobody

wanted them. So now the Germans volunteered to go for other townships. Now everybody gets $250 to $300 from the townships they went for and everybody could go where he wants to and get each $100 from the government and everybody gets $16 a month when they are drafted.

This is the third time that they drafted, but the first two times, one was free if one would pay $300. Nearly everyone would have paid it if he could scape it together but in this draft they could not, else they would not be able to get enough men. First they took the money, but now they take the men. Now you can see the racket they have here in America.

Across the north, German Catholics offered some of the strongest opposition to the war. They had the second lowest enlistment rates of any ethnic group, after the Irish. In Wisconsin, draft riots broke out in several strongly German Catholic townships.

Benedict Schmid

Schmid was drafted in the spring of 1864 and served in Company G, Second Minnesota Regiment—a unit of musicians. He kept up his habit of writing daily entries in a diary. His Civil War journal begins: "I was drafted on the 28 of May and reported at Saint Paul on the 13 of June. Went to Fort Snelling the 14th where I had to remain one week, that Tuesday we left the Fort for the South with 115 men." The army sent Schmid to Atlanta where his company was assigned to the rearguard behind Sherman's main force.

Schmid first learned of the daring march to the sea on November 2nd, when he wrote: "We have orders that we have no opportunity during the next forty days to mail letters, which point to a long campaign." Sherman's plan was to head directly to the Atlantic coast without any support lines. Lacking wagon trains, the army relied on food from the surrounding countryside. He wrote: Nov. 17-21: "We were marching. The countryside was very pretty. We live off the planters along the road. Sweet potato, we have plenty, but hardtack we have none." During the whole march, he noted, they received only four days worth of rations. One day, he was surprised to come across some old neighbors from Chanhassen. He wrote, "We remained in camp until the recruits came, among them…Schuler and Schneider as well as the Eberts."

Cut off from the outside world, Benedict did not hear from his wife until December 19th. It was important news. "I got a letter from Rosina and one from Mary that Rosina was delivered of a little son on the 13th of November 1864. They are well." They reached Savannah just before Christmas 1864. Benedict, away from his family, wrote on Christmas Day, "This whole thing is for the birds."

Schmid was not a war hero like Edwin Aldritt. He served his time. A few weeks before the final Confederate surrender, he noted, "March 25, 1865: This day I had my first opportunity to shoot at a Southerner as I was on picket duty."

The war was over. Schmid's regiment continued their march up the coast, all the way to Washington, D.C. where he participated in the Grand Review. He wrote, "May 24: We had review in Washington. The weather was nice and there were many people in the streets."

He hoped to go home but did not receive his discharge for another two months. Finally, on July 21, 1865, he records, "On this day at four o'clock I received my discharge from U.S. I took the steamboat home. Got home as it got daylight. Here is the end of this dog's life." He wrote in his diary that he checked the fruit and brought in the rye. Schmid had returned to his farm.

Engelbert Schneider

The war seemed long and hard. Engelbert Schneider didn't want to go. This was an attitude shared by most of the men in the township. His wife told the family back in Germany that, "If it didn't have to be, Engelbert would not have gone. If anyone would have given him $1000 he'd have waited until the last day until he would have known for sure that he'd be drafted." He was assigned to Sherman's army just after the capture of Atlanta.

There were hardships, especially for those that remained behind. Anna wrote, "I have been left alone with my four children in the woods, because my husband ie to War for one year, as of today, September 25."

She was forced to work the land with the help of the few men left.

Anna Schneider wrote to her parents complaining of her husband's long absence during the Civil War. She managed the farm on her own for more than a year.

This week I threshed 300 bushels wheat, 80 bushels barley and 200 bushels of oats. Have all the grain laying there yet…I have eighteen head of cattle and six nice hogs. I have very nice corn and lots of potatoes and rutabagas. At times I can hardly bear it. I have to console myself that I am not alone without a husband. In my whole neighborhood there are only two men left. The rest are all gone and every woman has children. My brother-in-law, John Schmieg, is also here and also will stay here, but he is not from our township. Erhardt is also gone. He was drafted once, paid $300 and now he volunteered to go. This township hasn't furnished any men. Habloth was drafted also, but he skipped the country. The single ones stay at home and the married ones have to go and leave wife and children.

Engelbert was mustered out only a few days later and returned home. Nine months later, Frank Schneider was born.

Theodore Bost and the Draft

Bost voiced strong beliefs about the war and would have seemed a likely candidate to enlist. Early in the war, he voiced a reluctance to support the Union because there was no commitment to end slavery. But there was little desire on anyone's part to sign up. After the draft was instituted in 1863, Bost was uneasy as each draft came and went. In November 22, 1863, he informed his parents, "The war goes on demanding more and more men; 300,000 will be drafted in six weeks' time, and I have very little chance anymore of getting out of it. So many men have been exempted on account of illness that no more than 50,000 were accepted out of the 300,000 [examined], so this time they're going to be less choosy."

He excused his failure to serve because the draft should take "the proper proportion of rabble and Copperheads instead of filling the ranks with good Republicans…" Undoubtably, it would teach them a lesson!

There seems to have been little social stigma to efforts to avoid the draft. Nationally, only seven percent of the men whose names were drawn actually served. On April 6, 1865, only days before Lee's surrender at Appomattox, Bost wrote that, "because the last draft was supposed to take the rest of the able-bodied men from twenty to forty-five in Chanhassen, we were virtually certain that we would see all our friends going off to war, leaving us alone with their Democratic and unbelieving enemies. Powers and Fuller have been rejected as unfit, and only Sarver was accepted. The last has been called up twice, and both times he has managed to get sent home by pretending to be sick. He has just sent his wife here asking me to get another man to take an oath that he, Sarver, injured his back two years ago, but that's something I can't do." In the list of sins, lying broke the commandments but there was no moral code requiring service in the United States Army.

Disputes on the home front

Theodore Bost was elected justice of the peace at the April 1862 town meeting and complained to his parents about the difficulties of the job. He wrote, "My appointment as Justice of the Peace pays me almost nothing, seeing that the Germans who get into fights with each other deal with their legal problems in Chaska where they can get liquor." In the summer of 1863, he wrote, "Immigration has abruptly come to a halt, and although the Dutch are beginning once more, all the German and Swedish Protestants are trying to sell so they won't have to stay in a county governed more and more by bigoted Catholics and Democrats." His views were sharp and the Germans apparently reciprocated. The cultural wars spilled over into the political area.

The draft forced the township into its most difficult political decision yet. During the Civil War, the federal government required each township to supply troops. Often, these quotas were filled with volunteers but by 1864, it became obvious that Chanhassen would have a hard time. First, deferments for medical reasons were given generously. Second, other towns offered substantial bonuses to volunteers in order to fill their quotas. A young man, facing a draft to meet Chanhassen's quota, might go to another town to enlist and collect a substantial bonus.

Recognizing the problem, the supervisors called a special town meeting on August 8th, 1864 to debate a motion "that the town of Chanhassen raise a tax sufficient to fill the quota of said town." The minutes do not give any of the debate but it is clear that the discussion was heated. When it came time for a vote, William Sarver, the chairman, could not decide the outcome from the usual voice vote. He ordered the voters to line up on either side of the school house in two rows representing the pros and cons. George Powers recorded, "Much confusion, discussion and uproar followed—the two parties being nearly balanced rendered it somewhat difficult to decide upon which side the majority voted & the clerk did not learn that the chairman formally decided the question." Sarver asked for a motion to adjourn but both sides had already headed out the door in an argument.

The supervisors must have been stunned. They needed to fill their quota but faced the loss of most of the remaining men to the lure of bounties. They gathered again on September 20th, 1864, this time without a general meeting. "The Supervisors met at the town clerk's office [George Powers] at the time indicated by the above date to take into consideration the exigencies of the case as presented by the fact that our town was called upon to furnish ten men to fill a recent call for troops and that by a military order those drafted could go and enlist for other towns offering bounties if they went before receiving a formal notice of their being drafted. They placed the legal justification for this questionable manuever in the town minutes.

> Thereupon the Supervisors believing that the town board was authorized by law to offer bounties to fill the town's quota.
> Resolved that they proceed to canvass the town for the purpose of conferring with and consulting the wishes of the legal voters respecting taxing the town to offer bounties to those who might enter into the U.S. Service for our town.

In short, the board took it upon themselves to approve a major financial obligation. Bonds were issued to raise the money—$2,833.

It was financed through a bond issue. Evidently the response was not sufficient because the interest rate was quickly boosted from seven to ten per cent. The *Chaska Weekly Herald* recognized the weight of this tax. "Never before was there such a levee," it proclaimed in its December 31, 1864 issue. "In Chanhassen the tax for all purposes is nearly nine dollars on the hundred." The *History of Carver County* states: "No debt was ever more cheerfully paid by the township than this war debt of 1864." But the evidence clearly shows that the debt was unwanted by many citizens and proved a burr in local finances for several more years. In the previous year, as many as forty Chanhassen families were in arrears with their taxes.

This debate over the draft bounties only exposed deep cultural, religious, and political differences between the Germans and the Yankees. In the fall, Chanhassen voted for General McClellan, the Democratic candidate who hinted at a negotiated peace with the South, instead of supporting the reelection of Abraham Lincoln. Lincoln handily won Minnesota but in the township, the vote was McClellan, 610 to Lincoln, 484.

A bitterness grew between the two factions, erupting once the war ended. Since they had established the township, the old Yankees had held many important offices, sometimes sharing slots with the Germans. The German population, centered around the hamlet in the northeast, began exerting its influence.

As the Civil War came to a close, many men from the township were on military duty. At the sparsely attended April 1865 town meeting, John Geiser was elected as Chairman of the Board of Supervisors. He refused to serve and the historic record does not state his reasons. In his stead, the board chose Theodore Bost as Chairman. He had the support of his Republican friends. It was a difficult year. The tensions created by the bounty debate spilled over into every local issue. Bost complained, in the end, "The salary...is the same as the wage of someone hired to load manure, and I would prefer to do the latter."

Samuel Geiser (1841–1926) replaced George Powers as town clerk at the 1866 town meeting. He is pictured here with his third wife, Maude.

Bost created enmity since he obviously detested the German population and it appears they reciprocated the feelings. Bost complained, "In many parts of the country people make it a practice to defy the authorities who ordinarily—not wanting to incut the enmity of their close neighbors—let them get away with it. Cutting timber on government land, working on Sunday, refusing to pay dog license fees, and so forth, were becoming more and more common, and I put a stop to it in spite of several people's threats. I had several dogs killed. This threw a scare into the dog owners." Later, he attributed all his problems to the dogs. He wrote on April 20, 1866, "The whole thing started because I insisted on enforcing a law."

To Bost's chagrin, the failure to pay taxes had a direct economic effect on his personal finances. He wrote on January 24, 1865, "If the Chanhassen people pay their taxes when they're legally due, I shall also collect my percentage as Treasurer and use it to pay my own taxes, but these are so high this year that people will put off paying as long as possible, with the result that a new Treasurer will be the one to receive them, since I don't expect to be reelected."

He predicted his political future accurately. The 1866 town meeting produced a minor revolution. John Geiser was elected as Chairman of the Board of Supervisors. More importantly, George Powers was tossed out as Town Clerk, replaced by Samuel Geiser. Nicholas Rosbach was chosen as constable. Accusations of forgery and theft flew around the township.

Within days they declared all the newly-elected posts vacant because they failed to qualify according to the law. It is not clear from the records which side initiated the action. Powers and Bost pointed their finger at one new officer as the primary rumormonger. The political maneuvers, Powers wrote in the official minutes, were a smoke screen. Powers wrote, "He and all the officers elected with him fail[ed] to qualify to divert attention from his failures and criminal neglect." Bost explained to his parents, "Powers and I have convened a meeting of the whole township at which the man who falsely accused us has promised to make a complete retraction."

Bost complained, in a letter on April 20, 1866:

> It is all very disagreeable, especially because our neighbors are more than happy to hear bad things about Christian Republicans. If it were not essential for me to complete my term of office in order to protect the interests of our republican party, I'd have resigned my office last spring, but then all the German scum would have elected a man who has no principles in my place. They have beaten us 60 to 12…

At that special town meeting, held on April 28th, 1866, the charges were apparently laid aside but not completely resolved. George Powers wrote the only historic record, scarcely an unbiased source.

The minutes read:

> Some discussion followed showing that if mistakes in regard to town and bounty orders had been made, they were hardly worthy of the name of mistake—that in the case of the bounty bonds

it consisted in canceling the wrong numbers by a previous board which cannot but correct itself and can do no harm. And in regard to the town order it consisted in the wrong numbering of one order and the consequent failure to record the same. The proof and explanation showed that one of the auditors had grossly neglected his duty in not meeting with the auditors in consequence of which they could not make out and perfect the auditors report—that on that account a complete state of the town could not be presented and that with matters in that unsettled state on account of his criminal neglect after being re-elected as Supervisor and he and all the other officers elected with him failing to qualify to divert attention from his failures and criminal neglect. He alone was found to be the guilty party.

Who was he? The records do not state. At the special meeting, Samuel Geiser was elected Town Clerk, suggesting that he was not the culprit. Henry Teich was chosen as assessor and treasurer.

At the April 1867 annual town meeting, the Germans voted to pursue legal action against Powers, accusing him of walking off with the desk from the town clerk's office. Bost wrote:

> The principal [accusation] against me and Powers, including thefts and embezzlement of public money, etc. etc. which our accusers said they could prove from the town record books. Not being a businessman, I thought perhaps I might have made some mistakes in our complicated bookkeeping, but after fifteen months we grew weary of these accusations, which were now taking the form of legal proceedings, so we demanded an examination of the books. For the eight years when we were "in power," it has proved possible to find only trivial errors (totalling forty cents) in accounts running into thousands of dollars, whereas just in the past year that our enemies have been keeping the books it has transpired that at least $40 have been taken which they will have to pay back. All our neighbors, both democrats and Republicans, took our side, and we have all contributed to make up a fund…to defend Powers in a trial which will not take place now…

This year, Teich moved up to Supervisor, replacing Ess, and Peter Bartel became Assessor and Treasurer.

To the great dismay of the Yankees, their vision of community was being replaced by the new immigrants. They were German, Dutch, Luxemborg. They did not gather at the Congregational Church. They did not debate moral issues at the Lyceum. They voted Democratic. And they drank. *The Chaska Weekly Herald*, after the state elections in 1867, showed that the Germans had won political power in the township, proclaiming, "Chanhassen has nobly earned the name of being the 'banner Democratic town of the county.' She rolled up a majority of ninety-one."

Theodore Bost kept up his fight for a few years. He wrote, for example, in 1873, that family members would be pleased "to see how severe I was with the German Catholics. You'll recall that I've been complaining that we're under the domination of lawless Germans. For ten years they've refused to prosecute the hundred or so saloon keepers who sell beer and brandy without being licensed to do so. It's odd to have to fight here against an all-powerful Catholic majority in this county."

Bost gave up the battle. In 1874 he moved to Excelsior where he attempted to run a store. In 1887 Theodore and Sophie moved to Pomona, California, probably following their friend, the Rev. Charles Sheldon. They remained in California the rest of their lives. In Chanhassen Township, many tensions would be resolved in the coming years through a new political arrangement.

Chapter Four
An American Schwarzwald

More and more of the new German Catholic immigrants settled in the northeast corner of the township between Lake Susan to the south, Lake Ann to the west, and Long Lake to the north. Soon, missionary priests began to visit the families, typically on a weekday and then only a few times each month. The mass was read in the homes of Nicholas Faber, located on Lake Susan, and Nicholas Rossbach. At the end of the Civil War, John Weih, Peter Bartel, Nicholas Rossbach, Henry Pauly, Peter Weller, Peter Schroeder, John Geiser and the three Cordell families formed a parish after repeated visits by an ambitious missionary priest named Father Magnus Mayr.

In 1865 Father Magnus Maria Mayr, O.S.B., formally organized the parish. They named it after Saint Hubert, patron saint of hunters. Father Mayr had strong views about the best means to retain the faith. He believed that the immigrants needed to recreate a German culture in America. The Germans, he wrote to a fellow priest in 1866, tried to become American in the first year. He imitated everything that "appears new, strange, and unGerman to him." He was soon "ashamed of his good and honorable German customs and ancestry." Germans who settled among those with unfamiliar "language and religions" were soon corrupted. "The old story of a 'free land' allows him recklessly to break the civil laws and still easier the church and religious laws..." Mayr wrote. German Catholics should settle together, worship together, and go to school together. In Chanhassen, he could encourage the Catholics to begin a small community centered around a church.

The first step was to build a church. Henry Pauly Sr. gave five acres for a church and the parish purchased an additional forty acres of the woods to the north. The congregation built a crude log cabin measuring eighteen by twenty-four feet. Some of Pauly's land was reserved for a cemetery.

The Reverend Father William Lette was appointed pastor of the parish in 1872. He announced to the parish that he refused to offer the sacrifice of mass until they built a new church. Many poorer families objected and left. Most families of the church went to work with their pastor to erect a new church. A frame building went up on the site west of the present old school. In 1877 Father Aloysius Wewer

John L. Geiser

Simon Cordell and Catherine Lehnertz Cordell were early settlers.

Gottfried Kelm settled on a farm just west of the village after the Civil War. Below: Anna Kelm

replaced Father Lette. He was the first of a long line of Franciscans to serve Saint Hubert's.

The new church became a magnet for new immigrants during the years following the Civil War. Most came as family groups including the Kleins, the Masons, and the Kerbers.

The Kerber family came to Chanhassen from Baden, Germany in 1872. They left Germany to keep the family together. The German government drafted one son, Leonard, into the army and a second, Dennis, was ready to be called. Unwilling to see their son go into the army, they arranged for Leonard to go to England. After the other family members joined him, they made the long journey to America. They had heard about Minnesota from an old friend, Wendelin Grimm, and decided to head to Carver County. The Kerbers stopped at the Grimm's home and then settled in Chaska for a year and a half. Franz worked at the brick factory to save money for a farm.

In 1874 Franz Kerber and his sons purchased a farm of seventy acres on the east shore of Lake Ann. The oldest son, Peter, purchased a farm on the south shore. They also purchased twenty acres of wooded land along Long Lake. Franz later moved into the village and served as caretaker for Saint Hubert's church and school and as gravedigger. At one time, Kerber farms surrounded the present-day center of Chanhassen.

Gottfried and Ann Kelm came to the United States from Prussia in 1863. They settled in northern Michigan where Gottfried worked at the copper mines. After a few years, they moved to Chanhassen and bought a farm just east of Saint Hubert's Church. Apparently, they

Matt Bleichner and Sophie Lebens Bleichner. He worked for the railroad. Their daughter, Mary, was the second person baptized at the "new" St. Hubert's Church in 1886.

Chanhassen Township, 1880

did well since they purchased another farm west of the village within a few years.

With many new families in the area, the parish moved to build a school. Father Mayr, after all, had emphasized the importance of a Catholic education. Father Ambrosius Janssen began construction of a two story brick building to serve as a school and a residence for the Franciscan Sisters in 1881. Within five years, that building burned to the ground and another school took its place. The new structure, built by John Geiser, lasted through the modern era. A wing was added in 1894 with two classrooms on the first floor and a hall on the second floor. The Sisters of Saint Benedict came to teach in 1895.

The Depot

The Chicago, Milwaukee & Saint Paul Railroad wanted to place its route through the growing hamlet that had sprung up around Saint Hubert's Church. Since the church owned most of the land, the railroad management was forced to negotiate with the parish leaders. The *Chaska Weekly Herald* reported, "It seems that the 'cut off' of the Hastings and Dakota RR runs through the Grave Yard near Saint Hubert's church. The right of way has not been secured and we understand cannot be without considerable trouble. The trustees of the church were in town on Monday to look into the matter. We understand that the Chief Engineer claims to have effected a settlement with Bishop Grace for the right of way." It was probably not contentious. Bishop Grace and then Bishop Ireland worked closely with the railroad companies at the time, encouraging Catholic immigration into Minnesota. In turn, the railroad gave increased prominence to rural crossroads and its church.

The railroad provided a connection with Minneapolis. Just as important, it made travel convenient to towns to the west such as Cologne, Young America, and Benton. The "Milwaukee Road" built a small depot in Chanhassen in 1882. It was, the paper said, "one of the handsomest and most convenient of any on the line." Nearby, the railroad built a coal shed. The building was modeled after standard company designs of the period. A young man, Henry Kelm, began learning telegraphy and began working for the railroad. In 1893 he was placed in charge of the Milwaukee Road office as station agent. He married Rose, one of Frederick Geiser's daughters.

The *History of the Minnesota Valley* commented on the town in 1882. The author said, "Chanhassen is strictly an agricultural town, there never having been a store, mill, or manufactory of any kind within its limits. The early pioneers did their trading at a town on Lake Minnetonka called Smithtown, but at the present time the people di-

Henry Kelm learned telegraphy and worked at the depot, later becoming station master.

The depot was completed in 1888. During WWII, the Milwaukee Road sold the depot to Joe Kerber who moved it to his farm just west of the village. The city owns the structure and plans to return it to a site near its original location.

vide their patronage among all the neighboring towns." The railroad changed the town. Several new buildings clustered around the railroad depot and the new church. The *Chaska Herald* reported on August 24, 1882 that, "This station, on the cut-off, in Chanhassen is growing into quite a little village. Peter Barthel has opened a grocery store there and his son Johnny has recently opened a saloon in the same building. Hubert Bongard has also opened a first-class saloon near the church and is doing a nice business. The Catholic Church Congregation is completing a fine school building near the church at that place and other new buildings are also contemplated in the near future."

Charles Dimler and Henry Mason opened a general merchandise store. Peter Feyereisen had a marble yard for tombstones, employing two men. John Geiser had a carpenter shop. The *Chaska Weekly Herald* reported, "[He] is probably the most busily engaged man in the place. In his large roomy carpenter shop, newly built last year, are constructed altars, pulpits, railings, counters, and the like, in very fine style." The Chaska paper stated that it was a fine shop of two stories measuring twenty-two by thirty-six feet. Willard (Dutch) Pauly was told that it was used as a hotel and that the carpenter shop was located on the west side of the street. Around the corner, Mr. Cordell had a store. Mr. Mohrbacher ran a saloon. George Bradley opened a store on Saint Hubert's Street. There was a social life as well. The locals, reported the Chaska paper, enjoyed the music of the local band. "Our band is filling the air with sweet music every evening. They are practicing for the Fourth." The men organized a baseball team.

John C. Geiser and Kate Riley Geiser

John C. Geiser

John C. Geiser was born in Arvilla, Indiana on February 22, 1847 and came to Chanhassen with his parents in 1865. He lived in Shakopee for several years, learning carpentry. Geiser supervised the construction of more than thirty churches and became the most popular church builder in Minnesota. His buildings include Saint Joseph in Waconia, Belle Plaine, Sleepy Eye, Waverly, Winstead, Jordan, Shakopee, Waconia, and Austin. He built Guardian Angels in Chaska. Although we do not have any of Geiser's records, it was typical for a contractor to take standard designs and modify them as the work progressed. His reputation grew based on the quality of the work and the personal dedication that he brought to it. The Norwood paper wrote, "Mr. Geiser is a faithful worker and an honest man and he has succeeded in completing many fine buildings and sometimes when he really lost money on the job."

John built a carpenter shop near the depot in 1888. In later years, Geiser and his wife moved to Deephaven where he died in 1924. In his obituary, the Chaska paper said, "He was a master builder, a genial, whole-souled gentleman, and much respected by a wide circle of friends.

Fred Geiser

Fred Geiser was born in 1856 on the family farm just west of the village center. He became widely known for his butter and egg business. On one occasion as he headed north to Excelsior, Fred lost control of his horses and his wagon overturned and the vats of butter went rolling down the hills. To many local residents, this area north of the intersection of Hwy 5 near County Road 17 is still known as the butter hills.

He was a great storyteller, remembers his grandson, Douglas Kelm. He left an intriguing legacy in Saint Hubert's Cemetery. Kelm relates:

Frederick Geiser (1856-1935) and Charlotte Miller Geiser (1857-1936)

The story he liked most is say, "Kid, you've got something to be really proud of, look over there in the cemetery, the biggest god damn tombstone in the cemetery and it's mine." It is still the largest tombstone in the cemetery. It says Geiser on the front and Schroeder on the back. Schroeder was Fred's sister's husband. His brother-in-law. Fred decided long before he died that he wanted a fine tombstone. He wanted the biggest one. It must stand seven feet or more tall. The story is that Fred looked at pictures when a salesman came around and chose one. It cost too much. He ap-

Fred Geiser ran a butter and egg business. His accident on the road to Excelsior gave the "Butter Hills" their name. In this photograph, taken in 1908, Clarence and Florence Geiser sit on the wagon.

*Below:
The two-sided tombstone of Fred Geiser and Henry Schroeder stands in St. Hubert's Cemetery, still the biggest.*

proached his brother-in-law. He said "Henry, I have a deal for you." The plot of land in the cemetery that is right next to mine is not purchased. You buy it. We will then jointly buy a tombstone and set it on the border. You will put your name up on your side and my name up on my side. How much would it cost? Henry asked. Fred quoted double the salesman's price. But we'll split it. Henry went to his grave not knowing that he paid the entire cost of the tombstone.

He began using the gravestone in 1935.

Prolific Lyman

Henry Lyman typified the mentality of many of the Northampton colonists. Their religious beliefs sought moral perfection. It carried over to his attitudes toward the land. Agriculture was more than a way to make a living. It demanded improvement. Lyman became friends with Peter Gideon of Excelsior, creator of the Wealthy apple, and Arthur Latham, president of the new Minnesota Horticultural Society. Mr. Lyman became a member of the society in 1891. He established an official "Trial Station" on his farm where he maintained copious notes on his experiments.

After he returned from a visit to Massachusetts following the Civil War, he planted seeds from apples of hardier varieties such as the Siberian crabapple. He grew a crabapple tree in his orchard that was named "Lyman's Prolific." It spread more than forty feet and became famous for its yield. He experimented with other fruit trees and grew one of the finest evergreen windbreaks in the state next to his home.

On one excursion with his son, Arthur, he noticed some fine alfalfa in a neighboring township and brought home some seed.

The period after the Civil War saw the application of science to horticulture and agriculture. The University of Minnesota Agricultural School promoted new ways to grow crops. Companies began promoting their new farm machinery, fertilizers and seeds in an increasingly wide array of magazines and newspapers.

In a typical report, Arthur wrote,

> I shall call attention to the marked difference in the behavior of two plantings of apple seeds by my father. In the year 1868 he planted a lot of seed from the Haas apples which grew Siberian crab trees and from his planting he got varieties of very small crabs up to hybrids as large as the Whitney No. 20, but not any large apples. By this planting was originated our Prolific, which is now a tree measuring forty feet spread and has become quite noted in the northwest.
>
> The year 1876 he planted a lot of Wealthy seed that were saved from a barrel of Wealthy apples that grew on three top-worked Siberian crab trees that were somewhat removed from other trees, the adjacent trees having killed down in the early seventies. By this planting, he originated an exceptionally fine lot of seedlings, which are nearly all of the large type of apples. In the years 1896, '97, '98, '99, 1900 and 1901 these seedlings have taken first premium as "best fall apple" [at the state fair].

Henry and Martha (Pomeroy) Lyman built their home (below) in 1882. It still stands along Galpin Boulevard.

Lyman farm circa 1900. Henry Lyman (with beard) holds the white horse on the right. His son, Arthur, lived on the farm and worked with his father.

Henry Lyman stands next to the original tree of Lyman's prolific crab. The tree was forty feet in diameter.

Henry Lyman built a new home in 1882—a substantial two story wood house with fashionable Italianate features. It is still standing. Lyman visited Massachusetts for the last time during the winter of 1891-92. He died in 1902, leaving the farm to his son, Arthur. His obituary said, "Mr. Lyman left a most honorable record, and the good he did in the direction of creating a pomology adapted to this comparatively new country will undoubtably perpetuate his name long after those who knew him personally have passed away." On his deathbed, he asked if the trees had been mulched.

In 1887 the Franciscan Brothers relinquished title to the property around St. Hubert's Church and a town was platted. Streets were named after saints. When the village was organized in 1896, however, they opted for the traditional name of Chanhassen.

Saint Hubertus

Archbishop John Ireland promoted a policy of settlement by Catholics as a means to build the church in Minnesota. Many towns were formed out of fields, often acquired through negotiations between the railroad and the church. Although Chanhassen was already a small hamlet, Ireland's influence could be seen as the parish leaders tried to create a Catholic community. In 1887 the Franciscans turned the property over to the diocese and platted the town of Saint Hubertus. They named the streets after the saints: Saint Aloys, Saint Claire, Saint Francis, Saint Joseph, Saint Mary. The main street was known as Saint Hubert until the mid-twentieth century. The church, carefully controlling the property, sold eighteen lots for an average price of $200 each. The new owners included the Cordell family, Mrs. Peter Schwader, and Joe Mason.

With a growing community and a new school, the parish committed itself to a new church in 1887. Not surprisingly, the committee turned to John Geiser. The building committee was headed by the Reverend Fulgentius Eich and included Joseph Mason, Secretary, Peter Feyereisen, Treasurer, Henry Pauly, John Simmons, John Mergens, Frank Drasen, and Fred Geiser. It cost $6,400.00. Archbishop John Ireland presided over the dedication of the new builidng in the autumn of 1888.

70　Chanhassen: A Centennial History

These photographs were taken in 1900 for the Archdiocese of Saint Paul. The school was built by John Geiser.

The Village of Chanhassen

On April 21, 1896, the thirty-five adult men gathered in John Geiser's carpenter shop to vote to incorporate a village government. The first officers were elected without opposition on May 5th. Gerhard Schroeder, a carpenter, was elected as President of the Council, John Rossbach, Bernard Zimmer, and Frank Drasen, councilmen; Peter Feyereisen, recorder; Nick Pauly, Treasurer; Frank Kolosky and Bernard Zimmer, Justices of the Peace; Gust Drucke and John Mason, Constables.

Why did they decide to form a village government? Some historians have suggested that the disagreements with the temperance–minded township residents inspired the split. After all, in the first order of business, the council granted a liquor license for Mathias Raser's saloon and one to Peter Feyereisen, Village Recorder and tombstone carver. But there is no evidence to support this argument. The majority of the township residents were from German heritage. The newspapers mention several saloons around the depot. In fact, the streets around the church had developed into a rural hamlet with very different interests. The Chaska paper reported that there was much activity after the incorporation and that all were pleased that the roads were better maintained.

Left to right: Minnie Rosbach, Elizabeth (Schlenk) Rettler, Anna (Schlenk) Pauly, Rose (Geiser) Kelm, Mrs. Schlenk, Anna (Rosbach) Schlenk. The children are Rosella Rettler and Martin Schlenk.

Mason and Dimler General Store. 1880s. Charles Dimler, left, and Henry Mason, right. Several small stores and saloons opened after the railroad came through Chanhassen.

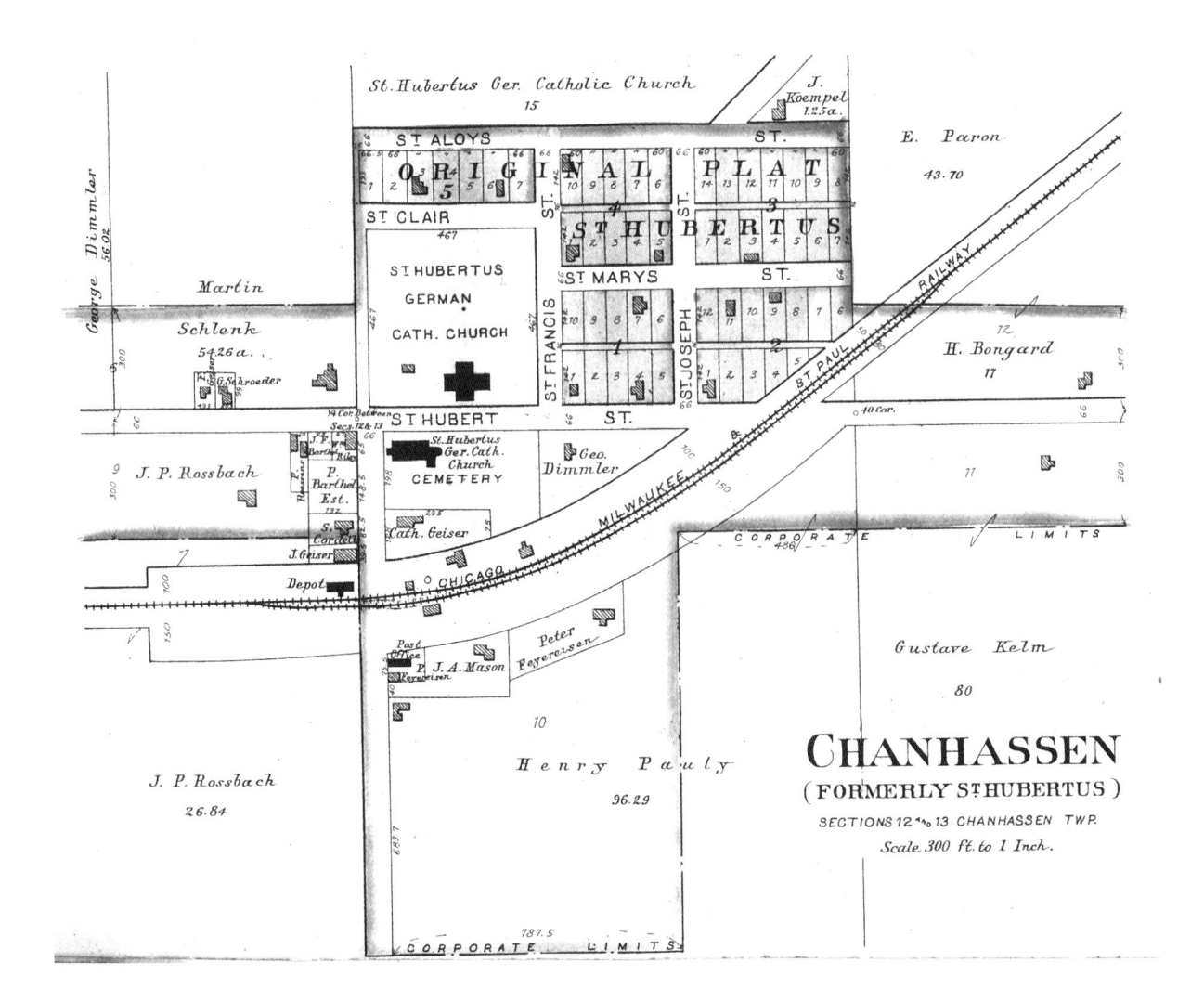

Original plat map of the village of Chanhassen, 1896

The village needed a hall to conduct its business. John Geiser provided the specifications and supervised the construction. The total costs were $4.50 for plans, $150 for lumber, $12.55 for freight, and $20.68 for labor. After the new hall was completed in 1898, the council approved the purchase of "a fine bell." In the rear of the hall, they placed a small jail, used, according to memory, generally to dry out visitors to the saloons.

At the turn of the century, Chanhassen had grown into a small hamlet around the Catholic church. For the next fifty years, it remained a quiet crossroads. Between 1900 and 1910, for example, the population decreased from 175 to 164. The township grew only modestly, from 1219 to 1368.

To a remarkable degree, they had fulfilled the teachings of Father Mayr, the founder of Saint Hubert's. At the turn of the century, a visitor wrote about his impressions of the new village. He said,

> Chanhassen is a German settlement and German is almost the only language heard among the villagers and the farmer folk from

Construction of St. Hubert's Church, 1887. Note the work crew in front.

the surrounding country who drive in for mass on a Sunday morning and linger for a bit of neighborly gossip before hitching their sturdy teams to wagons, buggies and carryalls and driving home again. You cannot walk through Chanhassen without catching a suggestion of its Bavarian atmosphere. It is, unfortunately, rather too closely connected with American civilization by the main line of the Milwaukee Road, but the tracks run through a sort of shallow gully and when no trains disturb the quietude the pedestrian and even the motorist, may imagine himself in some friendly settlement in the Schwarzwald or the foot hills of the Alps.

I think of people who complain because they are too poor to take a trip to Germany and wonder why they don't enrich themselves by adopting the slogan: See Chanhassen first.

After Saint Hubert's Church was completed, its members gathered for this photograph in 1890.

The interior of Saint Hubert's Church. Most of the altar work was carved by John Geiser.

CHANHASSEN: A CENTENNIAL HISTORY   75

Minute book for the Village of Chanhassen shows the rceord of the first council meeting on May 5, 1896.

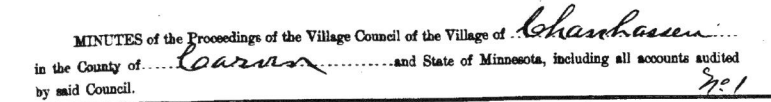

Gerhard Schroeder was elected as the first president of the council for the village of Chanhassen. Schroeder was born in Germany. He was a carpenter.

Chanhassen Boosters Band stands on the steps of the new village hall. John Geiser was the contractor.

76　Chanhassen: A Centennial History

This quilt was made by the ladies of St. Hubert's Church. People paid to have their name embroidered on one of the spokes. The quilt was raffled and won by Marie Leis when she was sixteen. In this photograph, Arnold and Claire Vogel point out the name of Susanna Hoen, Arnold's grandmother.

Women of Chanhassen, ca. 1900.

Charlotte (Miller) Geiser, Regina Schneider, Mary Lubbe, Elizabeth Raser, Anna (Mergens) Schroeder, Mrs. Ambrose Kerber. Seated left to right: Anna (Schlenk) Pauly, Abbie Pauly, Mary Jacques, Mrs. Peter Kerber

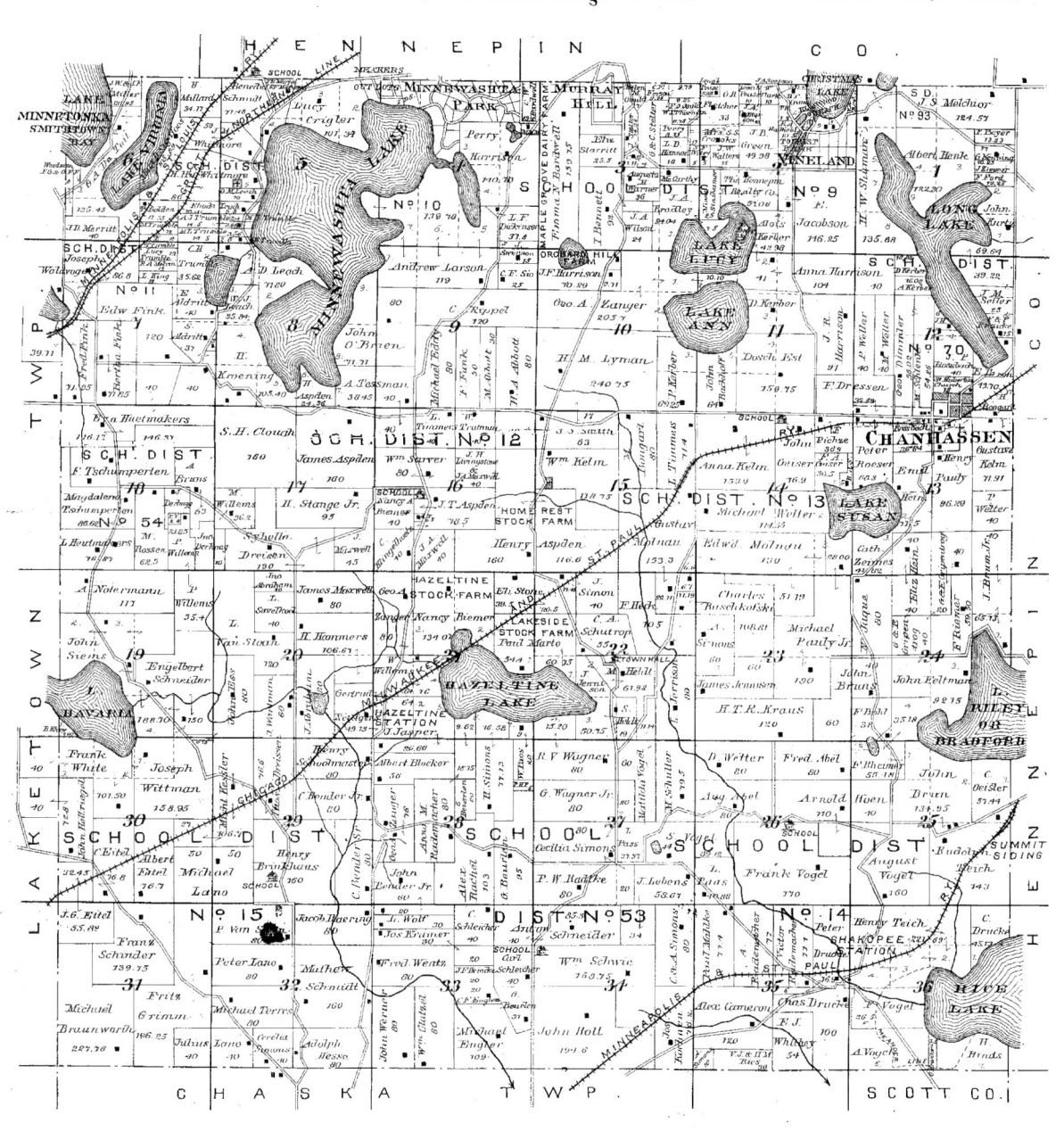

Chanhassen Township,
1896 Atlas

A Chanhassen Wedding Album

At the turn of the century, a visitor to Chanhassen recorded his memories of "A Rustic Wedding"

The ceremonies of marriage and burial are still the most important individual events in this changing world; and the rituals that mark their occurance are, consequently, the last to give way to changes that threaten to make human life one colorless monotony of system and efficiency.

The two streets of the town were already filled with teams that had brought guests from many miles around, though it was not yet 9 o'clock. Down every approaching road clouds of sunlit dust indicated the coming of more friends. The home of the bride's parents stood well back from the road in a shadowed, uncut lawn whereon men, women and children in their unaccustomed best stood in festive talk and laughter, greeting one another and bantering the tall young bridegroom who looked highly uncomfortable in a black coat with a huge bunch of flowers tied to a lapel with a pendant white ribbon.

The chatter and the friendly chaffing, all in German (including the laughter), the old land maenner and hausfrauen, who had broken the wilderness, the younger men and women who had left plow and churn to come to the wedding feast and the boys and girls who would be next to take up the beautiful heritage of normal daily labor, the flooding sunshine, the sweet May wind and the chiming church bells all blended dreamily into the remembered strains of Goldmark's "Rustic Wedding" music.

CHANHASSEN: A CENTENNIAL HISTORY 79

Top left: James F. Harrison and Nettie Bennett
Top right: Dan Kerber and Pauline Diethelm, 1920
Lower left: John Aldritt and Mary Witt
Lower right: Joseph Meuwissen and Susan Scholz, 1918

But now the imagined music changes to the melody of Grieg's Bridal Procession, for the wedding party is coming from the house. Silence falls on the guests in the yard and they form in two lines from the porch to the gate. Down the lane thus formed come two children in white with great bouquets. Following them are the bride's maids in muslin and ribbons, carrying flowers also, not only in their hands but in their eyes and cheeks. Behind them walk the awkward groomsmen, to whom no one pays any attention because now can be seen the bride herself on her father's black sleeved arm. She is beautiful as all brides are, with the right light in her eyes, the right happiness in her smile, the right spring in her step and the right calmness on the fair brow from which hangs the long veil, caught with orange blossoms on the temples and floating in the perfumed wind.

Her mother leans on the arm of her new son, and the little procession crosses the yard and turns down the street toward the church, where the bells are ringing clearly, almost drowning the songs of the orioles and robins who seem to have gathered in unusual numbers to make music on this happy morning.

All the guests follow and fill the little church during the long and solemn Roman ceremony, when the procession forms again, this time with the bride on her husband's arm. All return to the house and the yard, for the house will not hold them all, and the festivities begin.

For days and days the women of the family, even unto the fourth and fifth cousins, have been baking, boiling, stewing, and mixing rich German viands for the wedding feast. The bride's mother, protesting in vain, is put out of her own kitchen, over which she has presided for forty years, and is given a seat of honor on the porch where she is instructed to stay and keep her black silk dress clean. She doesn't enjoy it at all, and casts uneasy glances toward the closet where her big apron hangs and toward the kitchen where her neighbors and friends have taken impertinent charge.

CHANHASSEN: A CENTENNIAL HISTORY 81

Top left: Alois Kerber and Elizabeth Schutrop
Top right: August Sinnen and Anna Stelton, May 5, 1920
Left: Matt Schneider and Mary Notermann

The wedding breakfast begins at 10:30 and continues, in relays, until 2 in the afternoon, during which time more than 300 people are bountifully fed in a dining room that, at a pinch, will seat twenty-five at one time. Memory struggles in vain to remember the names of half the wonderful dishes served at that so-called breakfast! Even a German dictionary wouldn't include them all.

Out doors in the yard a platform has been built by the bride's father, forty feet square (the platform, not the bride's father, though the dimensions are ample), and over it a canvas roof to protect the dancers from the sun and possible rain. The band from Shakopee is coming at four o'clock to play for dancing, but bless you, eager young hearts and feet cannot wait until that time; so a local genius who plays the accordion is impressed into service and the dancing begins before noon. There are polkas, waltzes, quadrilles, and old German contra-dances; the floor is crowded to good natured suffocation and, the dancing once started, continues without intermission until five o'clock the next morning, the Shakopee band and the accordion spelling each other through the long, happy hours. Just beyond the dancing platform is a spotless new house, the bride's wedding gift from her father.

A wagon shed adjoining the big red barn has been converted into an open bar and here all day and all night, four husky volunteers open fresh kegs of foaming, amber beer serving it to all comers and sending great, dripping trays around among the guests in the house, on the porch where the old men are playing sixty-six and pinochle, in the yard and in the dancing pavilion.

For a short time in the afternoon the bridal party disappears and drives over to Shakopee for the important duty of having the wedding photographs taken; the groom sitting, and the bride standing with her hand on his shoulder. But they soon return to join the fun and country swains fight for the honor of leading the laughing bride through the mazes of a dance.

CHANHASSEN: A CENTENNIAL HISTORY 83

Top right: George Buschkowsky and Mary Jeurissen, 1920
Top left: John Rettler and Elizabeth Schlenk
Lower left: Leonard Roeser and Lorraine Jorissen, 1925
Lower right: Wedding party., probably Fritz Schmeig and Judy Reigert, at St. Hubert's Church.

Chapter Five
"The Garden Spot of the Earth"

EVEN AS OUR VISITOR WROTE about the quiet, peaceful village at the turn-of-the-century, he hinted that the times were changing. He tells the motorist, "See Chanhassen first!" Even in its rustic setting, the countryside of the township was now a place for the city-dweller to go for entertainment and recreation. During the last two decades of the nineteenth century, Saint Paul and Minneapolis grew into important urban areas. Trains, streetcars, and automobiles provided the means for the Twin City resident to get away from the urban environment within hours. So, although Chanhassen remained a rural township until the 1960s, it was quickly becoming a favorite place for a vacation, a healing retreat, a camp experience, or a summer home.

Governor John Lind is a perfect example of the trend. In 1900 he had just completed his third run for governor in four years. Following his defeat, Lind decided to pull up his roots in New Ulm and move to Minneapolis to work at a law firm. As a summer retreat, he purchased land along Lake Minnewashta in 1902. The *Chaska Weekly Herald* called the farm "one of the finest in Carver County." Lind, a populist Republican who bolted to the Democratic Party to support William Jennings Bryan, later served as President Wilson's emissary to Mexico

Governor John Lind purchased a farm along Lake Minnewashta following his defeat in 1900.

during the Pancho Villa uprisings. He wrote home often, expressing his wish to be along the cool shores of Minnewashta. Lind caught the Chanhassen tendency to improve his land, surrounding the home with trees from around the world including a gingko and a Russian Olive tree.

Alfalfadale

Arthur Lyman inherited his parents' farm after the death of his father. For several years, he had worked on the farm while teaching school in nearby districts. Arthur had the same keen intellect as his father and the same deep curiosity about horticulture. He took over the care of the Excelsior Station and began writing the annual reports to the Minnesota Horticultural Society.

In later years, he wrote about his travels with his father. He would recall one day in particular. Lyman wrote,

Arthur Lyman carried on his father's interest in agriculture, becoming the country's foremost proponent of Grimm alfalfa.

It was in 1880 that my father who, with his farming operations, raised some nursery stock, put in some seed of alfalfa, having first seen it on the farm of Tobias Ottinger near Victoria (east side of Pierson's Lake). Unfortunately, however, he purchased seed of ordinary alfalfa at the drug store. It came up beautifully and made a fine stand. The next spring, when the grass began to turn green, suddenly one day I asked my father: "Why doesn't our alfalfa look green?"

I ran down to the alfalfa patch excitedly, and found upon examination that not a single plant had survived.

Later, as a young man, I went to teach school in Dahlgren Township. Often, the children, in their language exercises, would write such sentences as "Chickens like everlasting clover," "hogs do well on everlasting clover, "etc.

And I found that the "Ewiger Klee" of the farm's of Dahlgren Township was a permanent crop.

One time, as I drove home from my school, I took some of the alfalfa hay, and any father again became interested and bought half a bushel of seed from Northrup and Braslin, a seed firm then in Minneapolis. It was sown and came up nicely. Surviving the winter, which was one of good snow protection, the next summer our new alfalfa produced three heavy crops, but the second winter it killed out completely.

Soon after, I saw a man named Ohnsorg who had a nice field. I asked him:

"How is your 'Ewiger Klee?'," supposing it had suffered the same fate as ours.

He replied, "I cut him three times." When I told him of ours killing he said, "I lose me no one plant."

This was the spring of 1893. Again I went to teach school in a neighboring township. One day I was talking with a farmer named Bade. He pointed to a distant hillside.

"Do you see that fence?" he asked.

"Yes."

"Do you see the beautiful green alfalfa on the left side of the fence? That is Kempke's field. Kempke and I planted alfalfa the same day, on land prepared exactly the same. Now Kempke's field is O. K. and mine is all gone."

By this time, having watched the everlasting clover for years, a light began to dawn upon me, and I said to him: "Where did you get your seed?"

"At the drug store," he said.

"And where did Kempke get his?"

"From Wendelin Grimm's," he said.

And I remembered how then Mr. Bade's face lighted up. He believed that he had found the solution of his problem, and I thought so, too.

The "everlasting clover" stuck in Arthur's mind. In 1893 he heard that Christian Bender, a Chanhassen farmer, had threshed six bushels of alfalfa seed to the acre on his place near Lake Bavaria. Henry bought some seed and planted it just northeast of the house. It grew for fourteen years. Arthur continued his investigations in the face of skepticism. After all, several progressive farm journals suggested that alfalfa could not be grown in Minnesota—except in Carver County where the soil was unique. Lyman found that the good fields were planted with seeds provided by a man named Wendelin Grimm.

Looking east across Lyman's field to the Joe Kerber farmstead and the District 13 school house. The school house was located were Paisley Park is today.

Lyman's Grimm ALFALFA

Arthur Lyman was an invenerate promoter for Grimm Alfalfa. He was the person most responsible for its widespread use in the 1920s and 1930s.

SCENE ON ALFALFADALE FARM
EXCELSIOR MINN.

GRIMM ALFALFA   A.B. LYMAN, PROP.

Lyman began a crusade to spread the use of this man's seed, using his connections with the Minnesota Horticultural Society. At a picnic excursion on Lake Minnetonka in 1900, he cornered Professor Willet M. Hays, head of the Agricultural Experiment Station at the University of Minnesota. Hays was intrigued and apparently trusted Lyman's opinion. Accompanied by an assistant, Professor Andrew Boss, the professor drove to Chanhassen. Lyman served as a guide during a three-day inspection that convinced Hays that they had found an important discovery. Hays agreed to begin plant trials at the experiment station, telling Lyman, "This marks the beginning of alfalfa in Minnesota."

Of course, the German farmers of Carver County had known about Grimm's Alfalfa for some time. The difference is that Lyman was connected to the developing "agribusiness" of Minnesota. He knew Hays and other professors at the University of Minnesota. He read the latest farm journals that promoted new approaches to agriculture. Furthermore, Lyman was located in a perfect spot. Chanhassen was farm land but it was farm land on the edge of the city. The promoters and professors could easily visit his farm.

To help with the experiments, Lyman obtained as much seed as possible by growing more than 100 acres of alfalfa. Although two cold, rainy seasons slowed the work, the third year produced a bumper crop. Other agriculture experiment stations become interested in Hays' and Lyman's new seed.

In 1904 Lyman and Hays decided to spring their new seed on the general market. To establish their credibility, they decided to target the agricultural elite of the state. Lyman presented a paper to the annual meeting of the Minnesota State Agricultural Society, held January 12, 1904 at the Masonic Temple in Minneapolis. A sharp question-and-answer session followed the presentation. In the audience, William J. Spellman of the United States Department of Agriculture (USDA) listened carefully and was convinced. He told the audience, "I cannot help but be impressed with this paper read by Mr. Lyman....[it is] of vital importance to the future of agriculture in....Minnesota and the Dakotas. We have been searching the world for a variety of alfalfa that would do just what this variety does. We sent a man to Turkestan (in then-imperial Russia) this summer at great expense to get something of that kind, but here we know we have what we sought." Spellman returned to Washington. Lyman wrote of the response:

A young Dick Lyman inspects Grimm Alfalfa.

> There was sent to Minnesota an expert investigator, Chas. J. Brand, later chief of the Bureau of Markets. He studied the question at length for months, tracing the origin of the seed of different fields all over the country, studying the habits of growth of the plant, the appearance of the seed, the color of the blossoms, and every other characteristic.
>
> Indicating how little most of us really see was the answer to his question made by a farmer who had raised Grimm alfalfa for 20 years.

"What is the color of the blossoms?"

"They are all purple," the farmer replied.

Yet when he and Mr. Brand went out to the field, the owner was more astonished than his visitor to find that they were variegated, a characteristic of the Grimm variety.

The USDA gave the seed its approval and paid for additional experiments. Hays, already widely respected in the field, was appointed assistant secretary of agriculture.

With acceptance from the movers and shakers and armed with favorable advertising quotes, Lyman and Hays began a promotional campaign. The crop needed a name. Hays officially named it "Grimm Alfalfa" in a bulletin in March 1904. Lyman called his product Lyman's Grimm Alfalfa Seed. The name was both a tribute to the farmer and a marketing ploy. The almost mythical story of the German farmer from Carver County connected with the average farmer. Lyman retold his story in dozens of magazine articles over the next two decades. He helped enshrine Grimm's farm through the formation of the Wendelin Grimm Association. This group placed a historic marker commemorating Grimm's farm in the 1920s. The publicity only helped establish the importance of Lyman's Grimm Alfalfa.

While other seed companies sold Grimm alfalfa, Lyman built his career on it. His farm became known as "Alfalfadale," A rapt correspondent for the *Orange Judd Farmer* visited Chanhassen, describing Alfalfadale as "a large roomy old-fashioned house built mainly for comfort and seems to speak a welcome even before the genial host and hostess open the door." Most of the seed, however, came from other farms that Lyman owned or through production agreements with other farmers. One publication said that in 1915, he sold $25,000 worth of seed. He filled his promotional brochures with testimonials. "Men drive for miles to see my thirty-acre field of Grimm…," wrote H.S. Schurtz from Three Rivers, Michigan. "We reluctantly paid A.B. Lyman $39.00 for a bushel of Grimm seed but we had the satisfaction of seeing alfalfa coming through the second winter heavier and better than the first cutting," wrote the James Risk Company from Dutchess County, New York.

How important was the discovery of Grimm's alfalfa? Minnesota's alfalfa acreage increased from 658 acres in 1900, to 2,288 in 1910, 45,419 in 1920, and 702,578 in 1930. By the 1930s, however, further experimentation in alternative seed, combined with the depression, led to a decline in the use of Arthur Lyman's Grimm Alfalfa. Lyman had suffered an illness while visiting a farm in Idaho and turned the management of the farm over to his son, Richard. By the 1940s, the family farm was used for raising sheep and turkeys.

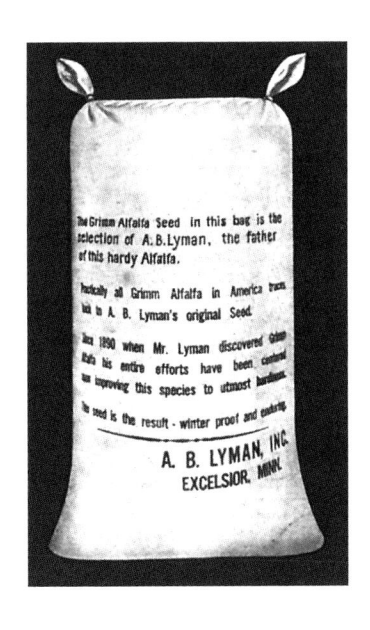

Main Building at the Minnesota Experimental Farm.

Experimental Farm

In 1907 the Minnesota Horticultural Society requested the state legislature to use $16,000 from the sale of the Excelsior Fruit Farm at Lake Minnetonka to purchase a new experimental farm and to provide $2,000 a year for maintenance. The bill passed with all provisions. When the administration of the Saint Paul Agricultural School began its search for the property, they recognized that land would be expensive near their campus. It appears that students and nearby residents stole fruit off the trees. These problems forced them to look to the country for the farm.

In the summer of 1907, they purchased eighty acres of land from Daniel and Bertha Fink of Chanhassen Township. The name "Excelsior Fruit Farm" continued to be used for this new facility until 1967 when they renamed the facility the "Horticultural Research Center." In 1931–32, the Farm purchased additional property two miles east of the original parcel. This second farm became known as Farm 2 and the original Fink farm as Farm 1.

The Fruit Farm quickly established its role as an important research center. They established the Fruit Breeding Farm "for the express purpose of breeding hardy fruit trees for Minnesota." In the first six years of its operation, students and staff transferred some 15,000 plum and apple seedlings to the new fruit farm from the main experiment station at Saint Paul. They moved thousands of controlled crosses of apples and plums, pears, grapes, raspberries, and strawberries growing at Saint Paul to Farm 1 and transplanted them into the fields.

Between 1907-1914 M. J. Dorsey of the Department of Horticulture was in charge of the fruit farm while conducting his other departmental duties at the Experiment Station on the Saint Paul campus. Charles Haralson was the first actual superintendent at the Fruit Breeding Farm, coming from South Dakota State College in 1914, retiring on January 1, 1923. In 1919 William H. Alderman was hired to head the Department of Horticulture on the Saint Paul campus in the College of Agriculture and became the superintendent of the Fruit Farm in 1923 after Haralson resigned. The pre–1940 staff and faculty who worked at the Fruit Breeding Farm were few and active for many years. Turnover was low. When Alderman took over as superintendent, Fred Haralson, a brother of Charles, who had been a horticultural foreman on the Saint Paul campus, became the assistant superintendent of the Fruit Farm, a position he held until his retirement in 1946.

The farm structures were initially simple, primarily greenhouses. In 1910, three summer cottages were built for staff and visitors. In 1915, the legislature appropriated funds for the superintendent's home, the water tower and an additional greenhouse. The administration building was constructed in 1931. A summer cottage was constructed on Lake Tamarack for the department head.

Although ostensibly an educational institution, class instruction in fruit breeding was never an organized effort. Horticulture students worked at the farm while faculty busily managed their own experiments. The results were astonishing. Forty fruit varieties were introduced from 1919-1940, an average of two new varieties a year.

This is the most tangible measure of the success of the Fruit Breeding Farm. Varieties included:

Apples: 'Beacon' (1936); 'Folwell' (1921); 'Haralson' (1922); 'Minnehaha' (1920); and 'Wedge' (1921); 'Prairie Spy' (1940).
Cherry-plums:'Nicollet' (1924); 'St. Anthony' (1923); 'Zumbra' (1920).
Gooseberries: 'Como' (1921).
Pears: 'Bantam' (1940); 'Parker' (1934).
Plums: 'Anoka' (1922), 'Elliott' (1920); 'Ember' (1936); 'Goldenrod' (1922); 'Hennepin' (1923); 'La Crescent' (1923); 'Mendota' (1924); 'Monitor' (1920); 'Mound' (1921) 'Radisson' (1925); 'Red Wing' (1920); 'Superior' (1933); 'Tonka' (1920), 'Underwood' (1920), 'Waconia' (1923),' and Winona' (1921).
Raspberries: 'Chief' (1930); 'Latham' (1920).
Strawberries: 'Chaska' (1921); 'Deephaven' (1921); 'Duluth' (1920); 'Easypicker' (1921); 'Minnehaha' (1920); 'Minnesota' (1920); 'Nokomis' (1921).
Ornamentals: 'Flame' crabapple (1934); 'Manitou' almond (1923); and 'Newport' plum (1923).

We still enjoy the fruits of their labor. The Haralson apple, introduced in 1922, is the most important apple variety ever developed in Minnesota. The Latham raspberry (1920) has been called "probably the most valued fruit introduction of the Fruit Breeding Farm." The plants are quite hardy and productive with nearly thorn free canes. Fruits are large, bright red and of good quality for home and commercial use. The Parker pear (1934) is still popular in Minnesota. The fruit is large, medium yellow with tender juicy sweet taste of very good quality. The Superior plum (1933) is a vigorous tree which bears at a young age and is a popular yard tree. Fruits are dark red with flesh rich yellow, firm, and popular for fresh use or jellies. Underwood plums (1920) are hardy, vigorous, and productive with large fruits, dark red, with yellow flesh and good for fresh use or jellies. Chief (1930) raspberries are very hardy and productive with medium sized fruits.

Its history is scarcely over. In recent years the farm released a new popular apple variety called the "Honeycrisp." Jim Luby, writing a few years ago, said,

> Today it is truly a center for all disciplines of horticultural research. Currently, research efforts include the breeding of woody ornamentals, development of more efficient nursery management practices, establishment of cultural techniques for commercial production of asparagus, broccoli, and cauliflower, and the breeding of vegetables such as sweet corn and melons.

Tanadoona

To other Twin City people, the land and lakes of Chanhassen meant a retreat from the hectic urban life. It meant finding a quiet spot near a lake with deep woods. It meant a summer at Camp Tanadoona.

The Minneapolis Camp Fire Girls was a new organization designed to provide a female counterpart to the Boy Scouts. Camping was a central experience. In the first years, they held camps at alternating sites. Intent on finding their own home, Margaret Fletcher worked with Mrs. Maude Armatage to bring a group of young women to the local Rotary Club in the summer of 1923. Their program, depicting a day at camp, inspired the Rotarians and they began a joint campaign to find a site.

In 1924, the Camp Fire Girls purchased Governor Lind's mansion and sixty-three acres on Lake Minnewashta and named it, "Tanadoona," a pseudo-Indian word meaning "Living out of doors." They gathered on the grounds in the late fall and the first group of girls almost burned down the mansion. Someone ran to the Hazelton farm for help and local farmers formed a bucket brigade and saved the building—losing the top floor.

Swimming in Lake Minnewashta at Camp Tanadoona.

Margaret Fletcher wrote, "First summer session was in 1925 although we had week end camps all winter long. The only weekends we missed were three or four in the very coldest weather. Sometimes the guardians came with their girls and sometimes Alice Erlougher, the office secretary, and I were the only adults. There were usually about a dozen girls. There was no fee as each group brought its own food and did its own work. We planned the program. As I remember, we had around sixty each session that first summer. We had to pack seven or eight in each tent part of the time."

Over the seven week season, two hundred and seven girls visited Tanadoona.

Activities at Camp Tanadoona. Below, campers create a grass shack.

Adele Coffin, a counselor that year, committed her thoughts to verse:

> Now those of us who were pioneers
> Have seen great changes thru these many years.
> The mansion of course still stands on the hill
> and the lodge centers most all activities still.
> The cabins of course have changed the most
> For that year no screens at all could they boast.
> Tents were pitched upon the board floors
> and mosquitos galore buzzed in at all doors.
>
> Down in the bowl the dishes were unpacked
> then up in the kitchen in piles they were stacked
> and cots were carried into each tent
> until our strength was practically spent.
>
> The National Training Course that first year
> brought many guardians from far and near.
> Miss Kempthorne, Miss Thomasma, and Miss McKellat
> suggested each cabin be named for a star.

"Camp Tanadoona," the brochure said, "offers happy, active, overflowing days under the guidance of well-trained, competent counselors. It offers the opportunity to learn more of the great outdoors, to share the joys of camp activities and wholesome comradeship." It was also a woman's world. A newspaper reporter visited the camp in 1938, writing, "I found it truly a center where healthful recreation and supervised activities conduce right living. Camp Fire Girls are encouraged to do well the simpler everyday things which make their homes happy and beautiful; they are encouraged to become efficient housekeepers and to take pleasure in their skill. They are taught to become interested in their community." If the camp philosophy seemed to teach old-fashioned feminine virtues, it also provided the girls important role-models of women running a camp with little masculine intrusion.

The magic of Tanadoona is found in its traditions and rituals. Karen Daniels, a camp counselor, kept her diary during the 1931 season. She wrote about two typical days:

> Friday July 19: The older girls planned a supper hike. There was no afternoon swim. Campers assembled at 5 and were divided into two groups. Catholics had "salmon wiggle" while others had "rum tum tiddy" (fried bacon, salmon, green peppers and pimentoes). All had milk and canned peaches and buttered bread. The day was very warm, and as soon as possible, the younger were picked up in cars and given a ride to the pasture. A storm came during supper and the program of games was abandoned for a hasty hike back. A heavy rain broke up dancing in the lodge. Tents were prepared for the night.

> Thursday, July 23: Telegram arrived yesterday, purported to have come from Santa Claus, announcing time would be today instead of the 25th. Hobby hour devoted to the making of gifts. Every girl and councillor drew a name, for whom she made a gift of material at camp. They included birchbark canoes, picture frames, baskets, book marks, paper-knives, dolls, painted bowls,

Counselors gather in front of cabins at Tanadoona.

books, wastebaskets, letter-boxes, etc. In the evening, two marionette shows were given, including the Xmas poem, "King John Was Not a Good Man" "When We Were Six" by A.A. Milne and "The Signing Lesson." The newspaper was read and then Santa, in costume, arrived to deliver gifts. There was a tree (elm) and stockings by the fire. Stick candy was served to all. Later, the councillors had a barbeque of pork-ribs in the fire bowl.

In 1996, it is one of the few camps remaining in the western suburbs. Sandy Steelman, the current director of the camp, said, "There have been changes over the years. We have people who drive past all the time who say, 'I can't believe its that close.' They always thought they were going out into the middle of nowhere. We get these older ladies who come by and tell stories about the twenties and thirties. They come up to me and start singing songs."

Mudcura

While some tilled the fertile soil of Chanhassen, others rolled around in it at a health spa known as Mudcura. Dr. Henry Fischer was born in Ontario, Canada and graduated from the Detroit Medical College. After graduation, he moved to Shakopee where he practiced medicine for several years. One day, a patient told Fischer about a spring on the Chanhassen side of the river. The doctor was intrigued and visited the site. The air was heavy with sulphur.

Fischer had read about the curative powers of sulphur mud. Several popular journals of the day touted the benefits of a mud treatment and Rosendahl Sulphur Springs (later known as Mudbaden) had just opened its doors in Jordan. Although it was a fad of the day, it probably did marginal good for sufferers of arthritis and rheumatism. Fischer bought the property. With Dr. Thenus M. Larsen of Jordan

Mudcura

Dr. Henry Fischer and his family. Left to right: Henry, Marie, Georgina, Jerome, Minnie and Antoinette.

and Fred W. Goodrich of Eden Prairie, he incorporated the Shakopee Mineral Springs Co. to "construct, operate and maintain a sanatorium for the accommodation and treatment of patients, especially those suffering from rheumatism and skin, kidney and nerve diseases." Dr. Fischer was corporate president, Dr. Larsen vice president, and Mr. Goodrich secretary-treasurer. Larsen was an important player since he was on the staff of the Mudbaden Sanitorium in Jordan at the time.

Mudcura opened on July 26, 1909. Fischer hired Fred Geiser to come down from Chanhassen to construct the main building. It offered special attention to its prospective customers, including twenty-seven rooms, a cigar and news stand, smoking room, and barber shop. The price was $15 to $25 per week, depending on the location of the room. In 1911 Dr. Fischer's residence was built. In 1912 a three-story addition was built on the main building to hold the guests and a third story was placed on the original structure. In 1913 the company built a twenty-six-room dormitory, bringing the capacity of the sanatorium to 100 patients. When they opened the doors, a contemporary article said, they had "four inmates requiring and ready to receive treatment."

What they came for was "the cure." Dr. Fischer's biography says that, "the soil surrounding the spring is so impregnated with sulphur and other mineral substances that when it is heated it throws off a strong odor." Undoubtably, the medicinal odor contributed to the psychological cure. Treatment began with a full doctor's examination by Dr. B.F. Pearson, a Shakopee doctor who worked at Mudcura. Pearson claimed that most came for some form of arthritis or sciatica and the hot mud probably did ease their pains.

Architect's rendering of the new Shakopee Mineral Springs Sanatorium. A third story was added within a few years.

Left: The friendly staff of Mudcura welcomes you!

Below: Mud was carted to the main building each morning for processing.

Every morning, the staff brought wagon loads of soil to the main building. They unloaded the mud into the basement then hauled it into a work room where it was prepared using machinery that softened and pulverized the mud. Next, the mud was steamed and moistened until it was of the proper consistency.

Treatments began at 6:00 a.m. Florence Greening, who worked at the sanitarium, said some North Dakota farmers who were patients would be ready and waiting by 5:30 a.m.. In the regular treatment the patient would strip, then lie on a sheet of canvas. Mud was packed all around and the canvas closed up to maintain the heat. The treatment usually lasted a half hour. In later years, patients sat in metal tubs and the mud was poured over them. Harold Kerber remembers sitting in the tub as a young boy, overwhelmed by the strong fumes but comforted by the warmth.

The patients were unwrapped, hosed down and put in a hot sulphur water bath. After the bath, the patient was dried and wrapped in a blanket to cool off. They received a massage where, a promotional piece said, "the disease is literally rubbed out of the body by the best trained masseurs that can be obtained." They could then return to their rooms to dress and go to the dining room for breakfast. The rest of the day was spent wandering the grounds, playing cards, or reading. Some visited the springs and had a drink of sulphur water. Others took electrical treatments. The recommended stay was three weeks.

Spreading the word about the remarkable powers of Mudcura was important. During 1914, Dr. Walter Weimers wrote a series of articles for the Shakopee paper, employing that favorite marketing technique—the testimonial.

* Mr. S. Slimmer, the Saint Paul cattle buyer claims the mudbaths are the stuff for his rheumatism.
* Mr. L.C. Sutmar of the firm of Lindeke, Warner, and Co. Saint Paul says: "A mud bath now and then is relished by the best of men."
* Mr. P.S. Tiedeman and Perry Peterson of Verona, N.D. say that they would rather be in a hot mud bath than to be home in the North Dakota weather.

Top: Patients were coated in mud and covered in canvas.

Bottom: After a sulphur bath, patients rested, wrapped in blankets.

Patients came from the Twin Cities, Minnesota, Wisconsin, Iowa, and North and South Dakota. Promoters claimed that patients came from all across America, including Alaska, and from foreign countries. Among them were George McManus, creator of the "Bringing Up Father" comic strip with Maggie and Jiggs. It became a treatment center for alcoholics. Fischer's son, Jim, was an alcoholic and helped start Alcoholics Anonymous in Minnesota. Henry Dimler remembered that "Fifty per cent were heavy alcoholics and they were pulling the alcohol out of them with this mud, just the same as would cure arthritis."

Mudcura was a small village. Indeed, they petitioned the county once to incorporate, a move that was rejected. Claire Vogel said, "It was almost like a hotel. It had everything. It had a laundry, a dining room, and a kitchen. It was all self-sufficient. They used to buy milk from my dad." Her sister, Anne, worked at Mudcura. She remembered, "They had a big dining room and a big kitchen and a laundry room. They had a little coffee shop down on the lower level. [The rooms] weren't real fancy but the corner rooms were nice and large. The other rooms were just narrow little holes in the wall, facing the inner court." The Mudcura baseball and football teams played local opponents. They built a small golf course.

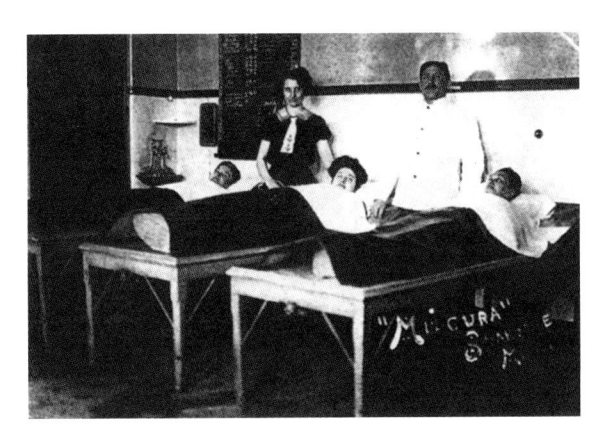

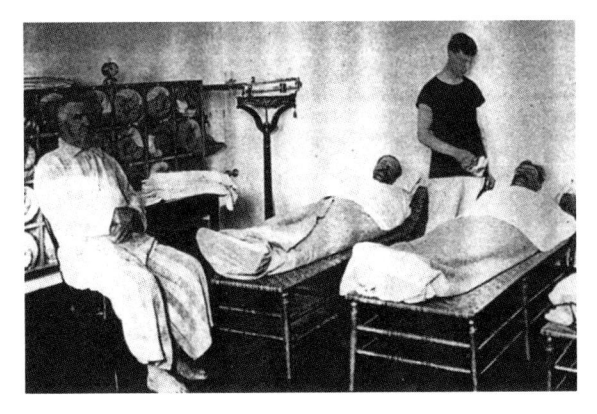

The Sanitarium hired local residents to clean rooms, move the mud, and cook in the kitchen. Anne Vogel worked cleaning rooms. Henry Dimler worked hauling mud. There were, he said, occasional problems. He said, "This German cook got into a fight with Dr. Fischer. The cook doctored the creamed sweet corn up with Cortinale and everybody got the runs. There was a building there just for the help and there weren't enough toilets that night."

Fischer was especially proud of his farm. In fact, Dr. Fischer was president of the Scott County Agricultural Society and vice president of the Scott County Farm Bureau. He won many state and local prizes for the farm animals. His Belgian horses hauled the mud. His poultry supplied the Mudcura kitchen. His prizewinning Holsteins provided the milk and cream. One of his heifers, "Princess Aaggie Polkadot deKol" set a world record for milk production—797.7 pounds of milk in seven days!

The cure lost its favor with the public and the number of patients dwindled. Fischer died in 1940. In 1951 Minnie Fischer dissolved the Shakopee Mineral Springs Co. and deeded the property to the Province of Our Lady of Consolation. The Franciscans transformed the site into Assumption Seminary and College. They taught classes in philosophy and religion with credits offered through either the College of Saint Catherine or Saint Thomas College. The brothers used the barn and operated a dairy farm. Students lived in the main building while staff lived in the doctor's house. When a new Franciscan retreat house opened in Prior Lake in 1965, the Seminary died, closing its doors in 1970. The buildings, once Dr. Fischer's pride, sit abandoned.

Fischer had this concrete bottle built over the spring—the source of Mudcura's healing powers.

Staff and patients relaxing on the grounds of Mudcura Sanitarium.

Charlie Peters and friend at Peter's Grove on Long Lake, October 27, 1920

A Summer Retreat

The desire for a summer in the country was an appealing dream for many city residents. In the midst of the depression, the *Minneapolis Star* offered a ray of hope. Arnold Chulik recalled,

> If you got so many subscriptions to the *Star*, you got a lot out there and they were small, only a twenty-foot lot instead of the normal forty foot or bigger. The result was that there were an awful lot of small pieces of ground that were not owned by the same person in a group. You owned one here and the next person would be from some other part and the result didn't lend itself to building too much.

Many lucky winners built summer cottages since not much fit into the tiny plats. The newspaper finished its promotion then sold the remaining property. Chulik said, "I bought in 1939 from a man in New York named Smedbeck. He owned all of this, the whole thing. He was kind of a real estate operator and I don't think…ever saw the property at all. My piece was 960 feet long and 100 feet wide. What I wanted to do was …buy this way on the lake, a couple hundred feet back from the lake and then 600-700 feet of lakeshore. He wouldn't sell that way because then that land in the back of my property would be useless because it wouldn't have any lake frontage. They cut the land into strips and we all got a strip." These odd lots would come back to haunt the future growth of the area.

Scraping dirt for a new house at Carver Beach in the spring of 1947. Edwin and Bernie Kerber.

The Carver Beach Association built a clubhouse where they held dinners and dances. A small store opened in the area. It proved a magnet to some of the local kids. Cy Kerber remembered, "Nelson's Store was right down on the lake where there is a swimming beach today.

102 CHANHASSEN: A CENTENNIAL HISTORY

Whenever dad would send us out into the fields to get the thistles out or get weeds out we always had a time to sneak down and eat a pint of ice cream and if we got big scoops we would use our big eyes and they'd look at us and say, 'Oh we'll give you a little extra.'"

Everyone had their favorite lake. City residents came each year to visit Kurvers Point on Long Lake or Schneider's Shore on Lake Bavaria or Leach's Resort on Lake Minnewashta. Ada Anding spent her summers on Red Cedar Point. "In the 1930s most of these places were summer places. The point was all cottages. The lake was not developed like it is now," she remembered. "We had bulrushes out front. We would get a nickel and we would go up to Leach's boat house and buy those golf ball suckers. Along the way we would go through the Leach farm and feed the pigs and see the cows."

The Kerbers rented boats on Lake Ann. Mel Kurvers recalled his family place on Long Lake. He said, "My dad had boats and he had a picnic table and people would come from the Twin Cities and would enjoy themselves on the weekends and have picnics. The people would share their picnic right with the cows in the pasture." Vinland, a small hamlet of summer homes, grew on the south shore of Christmas Lake. Most of the town kids preferred Lake Susan. Larry Klein remembered the day that the *Minneapolis Star* carried a photograph of four men who had fabulous luck fishing at Lake Susan. The next Sunday, there were so many people crowding to get to the lake that he couldn't even park in his yard.

In a radio talk in the 1920s, Herbert Aspden described Chanhassen as "The Garden Spot of the World," justifying that lofty title because of the work of the Experimental Farm and Arthur Lyman. The garden had now been invaded by the city dweller, looking to the township for peace, health, and recreation.

Several families rented out rowboats on Lake Ann. The cows provided competition.

Matthew Kurvers, owner of Kurvers Point Resort on Lotus Lake, shows his catch in the 1930s.

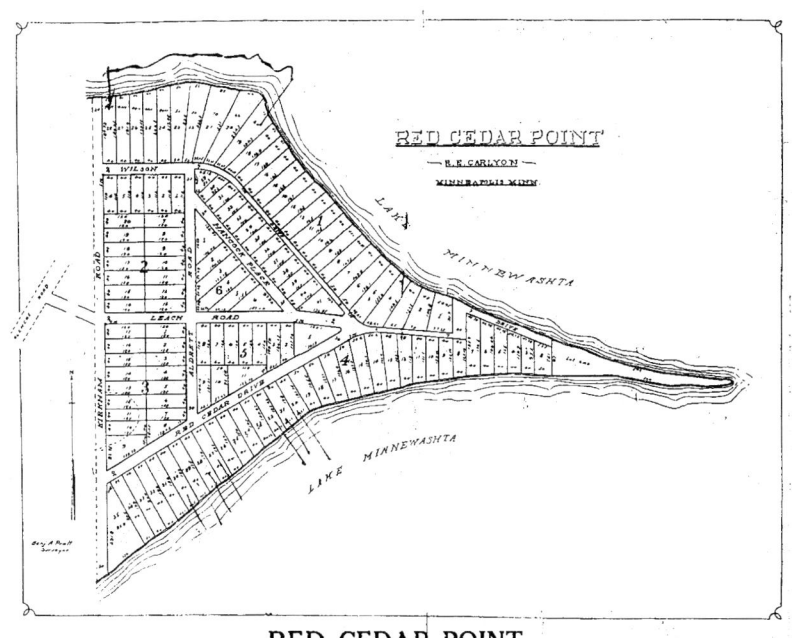

RED CEDAR POINT
Beautiful Wooded Lake Shore Lots
R. E. CARLYON, 315 Plymouth Building, Minneapolis, Minn.

Irene Richardson, mother of Ada Anding, fishing on Lake Minnewashta. She fished and rowed her own boat until she was almost ninety years old. The family says she almost always caught fish.

James D. Leach and Margaret Way, 1922. The photograph was taken at Leach's Resort on the west side of Lake Minnewashta.

Chapter Six
Hot Days, Cold Nights, Hard Work

Farming was the backbone of the township until the 1960s. It was also the center of daily life. "The dairy cow was really king," reminisced Cy Kerber. While the metaphor might have missed the gender, it accurately describes the local economy. With the growth of the metropolitan area, farms began to turn away from corn and wheat production to dairy goods.

Many older residents remember life on the farm. Harold Kerber wrote, "In 1913 my Dad and his hired hand milked twenty cows by hand twice a day, yielding a milk check averaging about $70 a month. Milk was hauled to Excelsior by horses with sleigh or wagon in eight gallon cans and put on a train and shipped to Minneapolis to the Northland Creamery."

Leander Kerber, who lived along Highway 5, remembered, "We sold milk to make a living. We had to use every inch to make it go and the machinery was mostly back muscle. There were a few people around that had a tractor but they were few and far between. In 1940, he bought a used tractor. It still runs."

In the 1920s milk was delivered to Excelsior or sold directly around the region. Paul Palmer said, "My dad used to have a milk route. He used to deliver milk for thirty years. He had four routes and

Threshing time at Alfalfadale Farm. Adults: John and Dennis Kerber. Children: Bernard and Harold Kerber.

Taking a break from filling the silo at the John Kerber farm, September 1943. Crew includes, left to right, Guido, John, Jerome, Florian and Charlie Kerber. Farmers would often work together, moving from farm to farm to complete this task.

us kids would help him during the summer. We had horses then. We'd bottle the milk here and deliver on our way to school. We had a big milk depot down in Excelsior. We used to deliver all around Lake Minnetonka."

By the 1930s, most milk was shipped to the Twin Cities Milk Producers Association. Emil Pauly owned the route but he hired Joe Kerber to drive the truck. Leander said, "Dad drove the milk truck for Emil Pauly for many years. If he needed the milk truck for picking up something, maybe the guy down the road had to pick up a plow, Dad had the privilege of using the truck for a little here and there."

Many of the neighbors remembered his daily visits. Tony Kerber recalls, "The first truck that I can remember that hauled milk was Joe's. He had an International truck. We took the milk up to Hwy 5. There was a milk stand and that's where we set the milk and Joe would pick it up and take it to the Twin Cities. We had to have two sets of cans. There were always two blankets in the winter that we threw under and over the milk cans." Gladys Kerber remembered, "Joe would come and…pick up the milk. We put it in eight gallon cans and then my mother would take a cup of whipping cream off the top. We had a tank with cold water and after that we built a milk house. When my Dad sold, they got rid of the milk cans and they piped up the barns for bulk tanks. It's pretty fast."

Riding Pauly's truck into Minneapolis became an important ritual. Cy Kerber was introduced to the modern highway on one trip. "The milk was picked up by the Paulys," he said. "I remember riding along with Kenny Pauly. It was the first time I saw a cloverleaf on the beltline. He kept going around the cloverleaf until we were back to the original and headed west again."

Before refrigerators, keeping the milk cool was hard work. The farmers kept ice houses. Harold Kerber said, "We had our own ice

Pauly's truck is parked on the north side of St. Hubert's Street by the feed mill in Chanhassen. Emil Pauly ran the local milk route but turned it over to other family members after the bar opened.

from Lotus Lake or Lake Ann. It had to be done in January and we cut blocks 20 x 20. We had a special building called the ice house. You bought saw dust by the truck load as insulation and to cool the milk."

Home

Julianne Kerber Hennen recalled her home:

> We had a wood stove in the kitchen and an oil burner in the living room which then heated the living room and mother and dad's bedroom downstairs. We had three bedrooms upstairs. Above the kitchen was the boy's bedroom because the heat from the kitchen went up there. Above the living room was the girls' bedroom which the oil burner heated. Then we had a third bedroom that had icicles in the winter. We had junk in there and the alfalfa had to be kept dry and the seed corn. There was a bed in there that we used in the summer. We had an outhouse.

The day began early. Gladys Kerber Schueren remembers a typical day, saying:

> In the mornings we would get up and help milk and run in the house and get ready. By the time we got in during the winter the house would be warm. We would get dressed and walk two miles to school and maybe one car would come by. When we would get home from school we would have to start all over again with the chores and the milking and then we would have to go out in the field and help husk corn. We would have to make sure there

Fred A. Molnau, Sr. with his work horses.

The Molnau house on Audubon Road was built in 1882. The house is constructed of Chaska brick.

was grain and hay down for all the animals and then we would go in the house, clean up, do our homework.

The whole family became part of the farm economy. Claire Vogel remembered that a small farm meant that everyone worked. "It was a dairy farm and we had to help milk cows," she said. "All of this was really, really hard work." Women and children helped with the garden. Gladys Kerber Schueren said, "We kept a big garden. We had red and white potatoes because the Russets kept longer so we had them and saved them for later and we had carrots which we put in the basement. We made sauerkraut. You would have barrels of apples and pumpkins and squash in the cellars."

Julianne Kerber helped with canning. "We had ground cherries, gooseberries, strawberries, raspberries, currants, grapes, plums, apples. There was always something in the garden and my mother canned everything. I helped [mother] all summer long on a wood stove with one of those big copper boilers that people think are priceless. I could care less! Seventeen or twenty-one quarts went in there. We did not go to bed until the wood box was full at night."

"They say the women didn't work years ago," Gladys says, "Don't tell me. They worked but they didn't get paid. They could not have gone to work. It was hard to get everything done at home."

Picking berries on the Lawson farm. Larry Lawson on right and a visiting cousin on left. The farm was located near Stratford Woods.

Hard Times

The Depression hit the local farms. On one hand, the farms tended to be self-sufficient so that poverty rarely meant a lack of food. It meant going without the extras. Many farmers faced foreclosures. Paul Palmer remembered, "That's when my father almost lost this place. In fact they thought they had sold it once and he had to stop the guy from plowing over here. He'd moved on and already started plowing. In the meantime my dad recovered this place. He had to go and tell that guy to quit plowing. That's how hard it was." "You could buy farms," one person said. "They almost gave them to you." Tony Kerber remembered the drifters coming through along the Milwaukee Road, "It was nothing to see fifty, sixty young guys at threshing time going west to look for work. Every once in a while one would come through the woods and ask for something to eat."

Finding other income was one way to survive the hard times. Claire Vogel remembered that her father started to sell honey. The whole family pitched in. Claire said,

> We had to milk the cows and we had to pick pickles and pick raspberries and pick strawberries. When we started working with

the honey we had an extractor and our mother would detach the wax that the bees put on the frames and then we would put it in the extractor. We didn't have any netting. We'd take the raspberries and we'd set up a stand on Flying Cloud Drive. I used to get 25¢ a box. Our mother started making sweet Russian dills and sold them too.

We came on hard times and we were going to sell the cattle. My dad took the cattle to South Saint Paul and the money we got …did not pay for the freight charges. I guess I always knew we were poor but we ate well because we were on a farm. I think I was aware of the hand-me-downs. But on a farm, we were self-sufficient. We didn't go hungry.

Henry Wrase, too, believed that farmers didn't fare too badly. He said, "I don't think farmers ever went hungry because they had the meat to butcher; any animal that they wanted and they had the vegetables because every woman knew how to can and I felt sorry for those people in town if they couldn't get a job."

The effects of the drought years in the early 1930s is shown in this photograph of Lake Minnewashta in 1933. A volley ball game, with Dorothy St. John, Priscilla Hobbs, Marie Puroy, Joyce Shaw, Ada Richardson Anding, is played on the lake bed in front of the Mayhew cottage.

The crisis in the national economy was deepened by several years of severe drought that threatened to destroy crops and livestock. Harold Kerber remembered,

A severe drought hit us from 1931 to 1936. 1934 was a very dry year. We had very little hay to put up. The grain was so short, it was cut with a mower, stacked loose in a pile, and threshed, and the straw was hauled in the barn and used for feed. The corn was so short that it was cut with the grain binder, shocked and later hauled in the barn. It was a few rough years for cattle as they were skinny and weak. Little pigs were worthless so a lot of them were killed off. The summer of 1936 was a record breaker as for sixty days straight, no rain fell and the temperature in the high nineties and over one hundred during the day. There were no mosquitoes and no lawn to mow.

The lakes were hard hit. Leander Kerber remembered, "People didn't seem to have much money to rent boats for a buck a day. The lake got smaller as the water got less and we had a marsh-like area on one side and during the dry years and dry days, we counted the cattle every time we saw them. If there was one short, we'd quickly run down by the lake and check to see if there was a cow stuck. We had to take the old truck and put a rope around the cow's neck. We saved several head of cattle that way.

Ada Anding said that Lake Minnewashta was down in those years. "You could walk over to the Camp Fire Girls and the water was ankle deep. There was another bar over where all the fish houses are now that we called Rocky Point."

The Modern Farm

Farming slowly modernized. Electricity was an important step. For years, Herbert Aspden was active in the progressive farm movement and headed the county Rural Electrification Agency. Through speeches, pamphlets, and radio talks, Aspden promoted the introduction of electricty into the township. Mary Lyman remembered that Alfalfadale got electricity around 1931. Harold Kerber's father didn't wait for everyone else.

The Lymans raised turkeys after the decline in the alfalfa market.

> My dad was a very progressive man, always interested in how to improve life on the farm. He put in a thirty-two volt home lighting plant in 1921. It consisted of sixteen storage batteries of two volts each which were charged with a gas-engine generator. The light plant and generator were in the basement of the house and powered the milking and lights for the house and all the farm buildings. It was the first farm in the area to have electricity. At a time when there were no bathrooms in Chanhassen, my dad installed one with hot and cold water under pressure in 1926. At that time there were no bathrooms in the village of Chanhassen.

The first big change came in the dairy barn. Cy Kerber said, "Suddenly you don't milk your cows by hand anymore. As soon as electricity came in. We ended up with a company called Surge but there was also DeLaval." But to Gladys Kerber, it meant lights in the house. "I was nine years old when I got electricity, she said. "It was five on Christmas Eve day. I remember saying now Santa Claus can really see tonight."

110   CHANHASSEN: A CENTENNIAL HISTORY

The latest and most progressive farming might have been found at High Path Farms. Harold Kerber wrote, "Charlie Kerber sold his farm to Daniel F. Bull, President of Cream of Wheat Corp. All the farm buildings were all vacated except for the house. The name of this was Highpath Farms. This was quite a show. All new farm buildings. Carnation Holstein cattle were shipped from the state of Washington by rail."

But the local farmers weren't always impressed. Cy Kerber said, "We bought our first purebred bull from Mr. Bull at Highpath Farm. I even remember the name…Highpath Ormsby Lundy Capp. Mr. Bull said, 'That bull should have stayed on our farm.' After we bought that bull, our herd in the Dairy Herd Improvement Association beat the Highpath Farm in dairy production." The farm is now the site of Eckankar.

Dan Kerber pulling a car out of a snow bank with his horses on Powers Boulevard in 1944.

Rovers Club

Farm life was hard work. But church, family and friends provided an active social life. The Rovers Club gave the farmers a time to get together and laugh. It began in November 1901 at the home of Mr. and Mrs. Henry Aspden. There were ten to fifteen families at the first party. For years, the club members met once a month except for the summer months. At their summer meeting, held just after the first hay was put up, they held a picnic at places like Schneider's Shore on Lake Bavaria or the school house on Highway 41.

Henry Wrase remembered,

> It was a family-oriented club. The president opened the meeting and usually we had to sing some songs. Somebody was always the leader in singing two or three songs. Somebody would gather the Rover news, what happened at the Kelzer place or at the Val Rose place or the Livingston place. There were…stretchy stories tied along with them to make it a little more on the comical side. Then the young children of the neighborhood always had their recitations or their songs. We met in homes and lunch was served by the hostess but only a sandwich and a piece of cake.

Willis Wilson was the popular auctioneer in the township. A member of the Rovers Club, Wilson handled their annual sale of picnic baskets.

The *Chaska Weekly Herald* often carried short notices about the meetings. For example, they described the 1928 Saint Patrick's Day meeting, held at the home of Val Rose. The entertainment featured Nettie Rose singing "When You and I Were Young" and several funny skits. Herbert Aspden, dressed in his green hat and green tie, gave a report. All eighty members sat down for a midnight supper. Olive Neuman remembered the excitement when they visited the

WHEN YOU VOTE NOVEMBER 8th

Remember that...

YOUR SUPPORT AND VOTE ARE APPRECIATED

By...

HOWARD OTTINGER

Candidate to Become the 21st District's

REPRESENTATIVE

In the Legislature

Howard Ottinger represented Chanhassen in the state legislature for more than twenty years.

Harrison's house. She said, "This Harrison had a phonograph and that was really something."

Once a year, the Rovers held their auction. Henry Wrase said,

> In the winter, when we had our meetings, there was always a fundraiser of some type. A pie social or a box social. The women would decorate their boxes and it was up to the men to buy them. Mr. Wilson, who was a member of the Rover's Club, was the auctioneer. He always had an auction at the box social and nobody could buy their wives' or girlfriends' box at a bargain.
>
> [The club] had their own plates and silverware that were in a big box then if the next meeting was over at the Kelzer home, then the Kelzer family would pick these up and take them to their place. They supplied some of the things at the picnics, ice cream, sunshine boxes, anybody sick would always get a sunshine box, cards, or something like that. Some of the money went for wedding gifts and other remembrances.

The Rover's Club disbanded around 1950. By then, there were many other social outlets and some of the original families had moved away.

The 4-H

Farm kids were expected to join 4-H. As Al Klingelhutz said, "It was really the only thing there was for rural young people to do." Edna Wrase said, "Back in 1951 our club was chosen the outstanding club in the state. We had as high as forty-eight members." Paul Palmer recalled, "My dad was very interested in 4-H Club. All of us kids belonged to 4-H Club."

Competition with other 4-Her's was important. Palmer said, "My brother was national potato-raising champion in 1924. He raised 571 bushels per acre and he was a state champion corn raiser."

One of the biggest thrills was attending the state fair. One year, Leander Kerber went to the farm boys' camp at the state fair grounds. "They had the county fair in Waconia, he said. "There was shortage of help at the 4-H stand and I worked a full shift every day and was chosen to go the the state fair. It was quite an honor."

Township Politics

After the village of Chanhassen was incorporated in 1896, local politics quieted down. It was an honor to serve on the township board but there were few sharp divisions. Frank Kerber was a supervisor for three years. He remembered some of the debates. He said, "By Pete Kerber's farm there was a creek running out of Lake Ann into the Geiser farm and we argued for two hours because he wanted to have a culvert on top of the hill. He wanted a culvert so the water can run from there underneath the road down to the creek. I said, 'That's the highest peak and you don't need no culvert there.' I earned $1.50 a day."

The roads were the only important issues. Arnold Chulik said, "The main issue has always been roads. Roads, roads, roads. The people that had them were opposed to paying for some other roads that they would never use. The big item at all of these town meetings was roads and getting them plowed in the winter. Many times we couldn't get to town because the roads weren't plowed." Florian Van Sloun remembered his service on the township board in similar terms, "Road problems every once in a while," he said. "It was pretty quiet around here."

The township did not have professional road crews. Everyone was expected to help. Frank Kerber said, "There were taxes that you could work off on the road. There were just a couple miles of road you had to take care of. The road boss would look it over. I earned $16.35 over two years time on the board."

Farmers were driving down those roads in automobiles by the 1920s. Many older residents fondly recall their first car—Harold Kerber: a Maxwell; T. Kerber: a '31 Chevy Coupe; Paul Palmer: a

William H. Kerber (Black Bill) farm was established in the 1870s by his father, Dennis. The property is now owned by Eckankar. To stop confusion between the two William Kerbers, they were identified by their hair color.

Will Kerber, Dan Kerber, Al Kerber, and Dennis Kerber around 1920.

William F. Kerber (White Bill) farm in the fall of 1916. Pictured are Josephine, Sophia, Tony, Ray, William F. (with horses) and Jacob (with spreader). Horses are June, May and Daisy.

1914 Chevrolet with prestone headlights; Leander Kerber: a '27 Overland purchased from Harry Mason in Excelsior.

Neighbor helped neighbor, especially for the big farm jobs. Harold Kerber said, "A lot of work was done together, the big heavy work like threshing, silo filling, and we would help each other. Women took lunch out in the morning and dinner at noon and then lunch in the afternoon."

The old Catholic and Yankee families helped each other out but there was still some tension between the two groups. A local farmer said of his neighbors,

> Everything below us toward Chanhassen was Catholic. My dad had no trust of Catholics at all. When my dad used to have them fill his silo, they'd fill ours last. The last time they had it filled, Dan Kerber was the head of [the crew]. Everytime they got done filling silos, Dan would go out and get a case of beer. He'd set it out and they each had a bottle. My dad came home from the milk route, saw the case of beer and he was going to have Dan arrested.

Although history books tend to tell about big disasters, political movements, and construction projects, the real life of Chanhassen is probably found in the small details and routines of the farm.

Chapter Seven
"A Village Small and Fair"

How Catholic was Chanhassen Village? The village voted 100% for Al Smith in 1928. Everyone was a Catholic except for the Mayor, a Lutheran. But his wife was Catholic! Little Rome, some people called it. How small was Chanhassen? Viola Buschkowsky, the daughter of that Lutheran mayor, remembered, "You knew everybody, you knew how many kids were in the school. You knew everything. You really knew them maybe too much." How German was Chanhassen? Lorraine Roeser said that people from other towns sneered at "Them dam Germans from Chanhassen."

Many of the families spoke German or Dutch at home. Julianne Kerber said, "When I started grade school I spoke very little English. We talked German at home. Our mother's dad came from Holland and so my mother talked Dutch and so us kids talked Dutch." Tony Kerber added, "The first two years we were taught in German. Willmar Molnau still talks German if he gets with the right guys." Henry Wrase remembered that it was a little different in the township. Although his parents spoke German, they picked up English quickly. "The main reason was living in this neighborhood there were a lot of English people—the Maxwells, the Livingstons, and others." Henry Dimler said, "I had three years in German, then because of WWI, the switch was made to English. When I started school I did not know English too good because German was spoken at home."

View of Chanhassen from the south, 1910

World War I

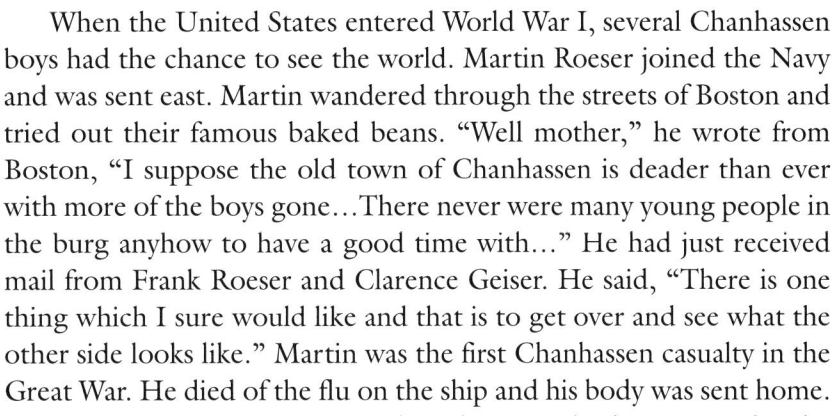

When the United States entered World War I, several Chanhassen boys had the chance to see the world. Martin Roeser joined the Navy and was sent east. Martin wandered through the streets of Boston and tried out their famous baked beans. "Well mother," he wrote from Boston, "I suppose the old town of Chanhassen is deader than ever with more of the boys gone…There never were many young people in the burg anyhow to have a good time with…" He had just received mail from Frank Roeser and Clarence Geiser. He said, "There is one thing which I sure would like and that is to get over and see what the other side looks like." Martin was the first Chanhassen casualty in the Great War. He died of the flu on the ship and his body was sent home.

Clarence Geiser, U.S. Navy, World War I

Lorraine Roeser remembered, "Everybody was out by the train when the coffin came and…it was carried right next to where I used to live." Some of the gathered crowd didn't think the coffin should be opened. They worried about the fumes and possible disease. Lorraine's father got mad. "He's a soldier and he died there," he said. They took the coffin into the yard and opened it up. The undertaker handed the coffin nails to Lorraine. "Sure enough when they took the things out, I could see him real good," she remembered almost eighty years later.

A year later, Lorraine remembered a quiet night in November. "We were alone one night, the men all went hunting," she said. "We all went to bed. Mother got up during the night and said she heard so much noise. She was just going crazy. She said they must have had a terrible fire in Shakopee because we could hear the fire siren. We didn't have a radio at the time. Finally we found out that the war was over and Shakopee was wide open. Finally, a freight train came through and they had the Kaiser hung [effigy] off the caboose with a rope around it. Then we knew we were safe." The war was over and boys like Gus Sinnen and Clarence Geiser would be returning soon.

Gus Sinnen in World War I

Prohibition

It should not be surprising that the village did not take to prohibition. After all, the local saloons were an important part of the social life of the village. Many families continued to brew their own home beer. Mostly, though, Chanhassen just ignored the Eighteenth Amendment. After all, the rest of the world rarely intruded on village life anyway.

Dutch Pauly said,

> It was illegal but the slot machines went wide open and so did the boozing. We had the post office and store. When they came to mail a letter, they lingered long enough to buy groceries. People came from miles around, the drinkers, the gamblers, the couples

A view north on Lake Street, Chanhassen, ca. 1910

who needed some kind of cheaters' nook. The place was supposed to be policed by sheriff's deputies but the deputies sat in.

I remember once the federal agent came and saw a couple of slot machines in operation. He called the sheriff and said, "come out and get the slots." Well, the guy running the Saint Paul House in Shakopee heard about it and called the people here and said, "keep the federal man there until we show up." He showed up with three or four of the most sociable talkers you ever saw. They sweet-talked the federal man and got him all boozed up.

So he loaded the slot machines in his car and headed for Shakopee. Now I don't know if you ever drove 101 to Shakopee but there's a big hill near the intersection down there and this guy was feeling very oblivious and went over the bluff in his automobile. The car goes smash, so do the slot machines and the federal man loses his job and everybody in Chanhassen and Shakopee is home free.

Where did they get the booze? The mafia? Capone? Red Jorrisen recalled, "Joe bought it from Emil Pauly. He bought it from a guy who was brewing it in his garage." Although the locals managed to avoid the law most of the time, sometimes they weren't so lucky. Red Jorissen got a police record at age fourteen. He said,

I got pinched. I was in jail one night. A ball player came over to Joe's because it was the only place that had pop or ice cream and they had a pool table. When Joe had more than he could handle I would kick my baseball shoes off and help him. This second baseman came over and said, 'Red, could I buy a half pint of alcohol.' I said sure from one ball player to another. Nothing else was said. Some other stools would come in and Joe sold them some drinks.

One day he came up to the house and wanted to go fishing so I went up to tend bar. About three thirty, four people came in. I thought they had a gun. They told me to stay where I was. They kept looking for things. They went to the steps and found a gallon of moonshine. I told them that they didn't have anything on me and they said, 'Yes we do. You sold some alcohol to one of our stools.' The baseball player got caught and they told him if he would give a name they would let him off. So I spent a night in jail.

The flagrant violation of Prohibition widened the cultural gulf with the old Yankee families, most of whom now centered their business and church life around Excelsior and had little or nothing to do with the village. Sometimes it went further. One Chanhassen farmer remembered, "My dad used to belong to the Ku Klux Klan. We had a cross burning in our front yard. This guy across Galpin Road, his name was Harrison, He owned that island down there between Lake Lucy and Lake Ann. There used to be a beautiful cabin on that place. Harrison owned the island and rented it to some folks who had a still down there. My dad was against it. He was a teetotaler from way back. That's the reason the Klan was here and he belonged to it. My mother didn't know from one day to the next whether he was going to be alive or not."

Left to right: Albert Pauly, John Roeser, Bill Pauly, Frank Lenardo, and unknown man. Ca. 1915.

The feelings were reciprocated. One old German farmer remembered with animosity after forty years, "All those Yankees. They never drank in Excelsior. They used to go to Chanhassen and drink and on the way home they'd throw all the whiskey bottles. They used to say they were blue-bellied Yankees in Excelsior. They ate dinner at 3 where we ate at 12."

Emil Pauly opened his bar a few months after repeal.

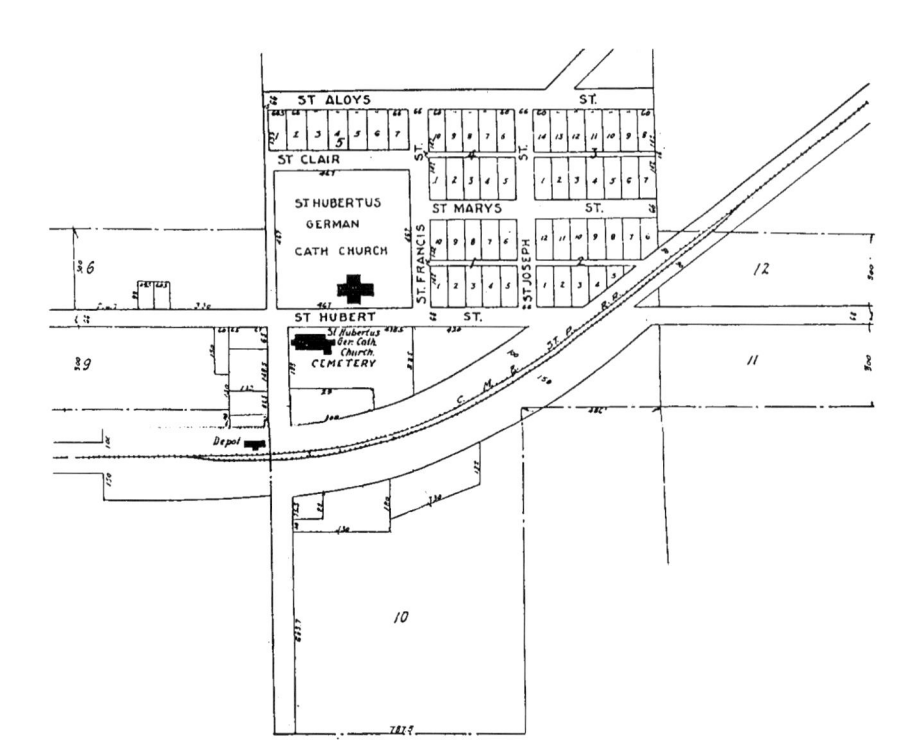

Chanhassen in 1929 from Hudson's Atlas.

Working on the Railroad

Transportation got easier. Many local residents remember walking up to Glen Lake or Excelsior to take the street cars to Minneapolis. Some people bought cars. Still, the most reliable source was the railroad. Trains came at 10:15 with the mail from Minneapolis and one headed to Minneapolis at 5:30 and then Flyers about 1:00. It provided work for local crews.

The depot was moved to the south side of the tracks when they doubled the line. The work crews camped in nearby woods, made up of many Italian immigrants. Lorraine Roeser's father was section foreman and so they were always stopping by her house. In a town where outsiders never ventured, these foreigners seemed wild and exotic. Lorraine Roeser said, "They brought the boss man's daughter presents. They brought me a teddy bear once and a bowl of fruit, which was something we had never seen in Chanhassen and my mother wouldn't even let me go outside on the porch. She was scared of them. She would say, 'Come in here right away, come in here right away. And would have the door shut."

She remembered their camp in the woods north of Saint Hubert's Church. "They lived in the woods," she said. "One of them went to town and got a priest and talk about singing. They sang really beautiful. We all stayed away from them. You know the women, some had women with them. They dug a hole in the clay in the side and they put coal in there and they pulled that out and put bread in there and baked it. Well we wanted to go see it. You know how kids are."

Railroad crew, taken circa 1904, includes Anton Schneider, John Schumman, William Jorisson, Ted Kurvers, Leonard Kurvers, and Nick Kurvers.

Henry Dimler said, "They put in another track and rebuilt the entire system. There were a bunch of Italians to do the work. I'll never forget my mother's brother running into the house one time when we lived in Chanhassen and they were after him with knives."

Violent arguments broke out among the Italians. One man was killed—his throat slit. They brought the body to the village hall. This was in a village where they only had a part-time constable and was remembered for many years as "the murder." Stories circulated about who had done the deed. Lorraine Roeser said, "I wanted to look at him. Somebody took the rag off and it was all blood, just cut all the way around. Flies were all over and the doctor was there."

The railroad provided steady work, though. Red Jorissen worked as a Gandy Dancer in the early 1930s. "It was hard work." he said. "Laying the tracks and switches. My dad was foreman and he had two men for the winter time. When it gets cold the tracks heave, so you have to shim it up so it is level. We had fourteen miles of tracks to patrol on an open motor car."

Stan Roeser, who worked for his father during the summer on rail crews, said, "Practically every little town had a section crew. We happened to have a twelve mile segment that ran from Glen Lake Sanitarium to Augusta. The first thing you'd do in the morning was ride the motor car the entire length."

In a small town, mail delivery was often the biggest event of the day. Rita Meuwissen Rojina recalled,

> Down the track a ways there was the arm. I worked at Pauly's grocery store all through high school during the war. Clarice Pauly and I used to work in the post office. We'd stamp all the mail and everything else, load the mail bag and then Lorraine Roeser came and got the mail bag and took it down there and hung it on this post. When we were littler kids, we went with her and the Flyer came and put an arm out and grabbed it. Occasionally they dropped it. Then you'd have to go pick it up and take it back to the post office for the next time. Otherwise they'd pick it up and throw another mail bag off.

It was a part of everyday life, Stan Roeser said,

> You gauged the time by them. I remember at 10:15 in the morning, we'd call it the Flyer and it would go west, it was a passenger train. That was No. 15. Then in the evening about 9:15, No. 16 would go east. Then in the morning we used to have the mail train, No. 6. Then No 5 would go the other way. When we picked berries on the Bren farm, we would try to have a crate of berries picked by the time the Flyer went by. That was kind of a gauge of whether you were having a good day or not.

During World War II, the Milwaukee Road sold the depot to Joe Kerber, who moved it out to his farm. Current plans call for the city to move the depot back to a site near its original location.

A Walk Through Town

"There wasn't much to do in town, said Lorraine Roeser. "They had Pauly's Liquor store and Joe's saloon. That was about all. Henry Mason had a store for a while but he didn't make much money. Everybody went to Pauly's because the mail was there. Farmers wouldn't come in to make two stops. We never had a doctor in town." If there weren't many buildings, it only means that those few are remembered with fondness by older residents.

The town did not get electricty until the 1920s. On October 17, 1923 a special election was held to determine if the residents wanted electricity. It was approved by a vote of 73 to 9. A bond issue was approved for erecting poles and wires for the village's seven street lights. Tony Kerber recalled, "They had electricity in the bank and in the store but not in the school or church at first."

You stepped into the country very quickly. The Kerbers had farms —White Bill and Black Bill. Black Bill is William H. Kerber and White Bill is William F. Kerber. The Sinnens had a farm about where the American Legion stands today. In the 1920s, the church sold off several lots in the land north and east of the school. Many of the existing houses date from that time.

Saint Hubert's Church and School, of course, dominated the town. The village hall was the only public building. For many years, the town had a bandshell next to the hall.

Chanhassen Boosters Band. Rear: Joe Klingelhutz, Alphonse Schroeder, Ole Kerber, Ted Kurvers, Director Herbert Stans, Eddie Pauly, Bill Jorisson. Center: Frank Roeser, Ray Sinnen, John Schneider, John Brose. Front: Elmer Kelm, Clarence Geiser, Matt Roeser, Martin Schlenk, and Walter Gripentrog.

Village Hall

Village Hall served as the official meeting place for the council, storage space for village records, jail, and sometime fire department.

George Buschkowsky was the pillar of village politics. He served as mayor from 1937 to 1963—thirteen consecutive terms. As one resident said, "He was like President Roosevelt, the only mayor we ever knew." Buschkowsky was also the center of Chanhassen's most popular punchline. He was a Lutheran—the only Lutheran in town and he was mayor! His daughter, Viola, remembered, "He was the only one the Catholics trusted." The job, which paid one dollar a month, was simple until the changes of the 1950s. Buschkowsky was a carpenter. One resident said, "He was tall, real easy going. He must have been a sensible man." Even though he was the town Lutheran, the mayor is buried in the cemetery at Saint Hubert's Church. Gus Sinnen was village clerk for more than thirty years.

The jail in back was rarely busy. Crime was limited to youthful pranks. Bob Meuwissen remembered his teenage years,

> Lawrence Schutrop was the town cop on weekends. He had an old Plymouth. He kept a hay rope in his trunk and he used to park down there by the one driveway by the DX station and watch people go through the stop sign in front of Pauly's. When he was in the restaurant having coffee, they took his hay rope out of the trunk, tied it around the telephone pole and then around his bumper. He was sitting in his car later and they went through town and through the stop light. He took off after them and the bumper just went…

Doug Kelm remembers the old Village Hall whenever he hears a bell ring. He recalled,

> A cousin of mine was visiting over a weekend and I was showing her around the great metropolis of Chanhassen and we came to the Village Hall which was sort of a playground for us because they never locked the Hall. The files were very open, shall we say. One of our playgrounds would be the back part of the Village Hall where there was a typical old fashioned jail cell and nobody minded the fact that the kids used the building as a play room as long as they didn't do any damage.
>
> But the Village Hall had a little bell tower. It was pulled by hand with the rope attached to the outside of the building and my cousin said, "Have you ever rang that bell?" I said no. I don't think you are supposed to. My cousin talked me into ringing the bell. Unfortunately, High Mass was in progress this Sunday morning right across the street and the windows and doors flew open because the ringing of that bell was the equivalent of a fire siren in Chanhassen. I perhaps got the worst spanking of my life because Elmer was at High Mass. I will never forget. Whenever I hear a bell it comes back to me."

The city still has the bell.

Susan Meuwissen stands next to Joe's fishing boat. Behind her is the village hall on its original location behind Pauly's Bar.

Inside the old Pauly store. Left to right: Christine Pauly, Mrs. Gerhard Schroeder, Henry Pauly, Fritz Pauly, Dutch Pauly and Albert Pauly.

Grocery Specials!
A. M. Pauly's Store
CHANHASSEN
One---Day Only---One
Wednesday, April 7th 1915

Frank's famous Sauerkraut large can only	7c
Kaiserhoff pear, extra fine per can only	10c
Chief Salomon peas per can for only	7c
Prize crop tomatoes 2 lb. can per can only	7c
Terrepin brand sliced pineapples per can only	12c
Maple corn flakes per packages for only	6c
Sunkissed rolled oats per package for only	18c
Sunkissed Macaroni per package for only	7c
Lenox soap 8 bars for only	25c

Albert Pauly purchased this store and post office from Henry Kelm. It burned in 1929.

Pauly's Store

Albert Pauly built his first store across the tracks. Frank Kerber states that it was owned by Peter Feyerisan who ran it as a post office and general merchandise store. It was later run by Henry Kelm. Dutch Pauly recalled the circumstances:

> Kelm come to my dad and he says, 'Albert, you've got to buy me out.' My dad said, I don't have any money. So he started my dad in business. He put $750 in his checking account and my dad was off. All these railroad men knew my father because he worked on the Milwaukee Railroad. He got all the business from these cook camps. Three of them out by Hazeltine and one in Chanhassen and one in Glen Lake. He got a good start working on the railroad and he learned how to splice rope and every farmer, if they would break their hay rope, he would go out and splice it.

It was destroyed in a fire on November 4, 1929. In this quiet town, it became one of those landmark events that every resident remembered. Lorraine Roeser saw smoke and called Annie Pauly twice, telling her that smoke was coming from the roof. "Well Annie went out and looked and she couldn't see," Mrs. Roeser said. "After the fire was over, the Excelsior guy said it started to burn in the roof. That was the biggest that ever happened here."

Viola Buschkowsky said, "I was sick that day, I was home, and I was on the bed watching that burn down." Clarice Pauly remembered, "People were carrying stuff. My grandparents lived upstairs and they had a dickens of a time getting Grandma Pauly out because she had all those possessions. She lost it all."

Dutch Pauly said,

> You could see the flames from Chaska. The firemen and everybody got stuff out of the store. Years ago you had to buy all your canned goods for the season. We just got the basement full up to the ceiling with canned goods and Fritz and I just got through filling the coal bin full and the stuff was standing out with the sales on the south side of the store and we drove off, got that away from the fire and saved that. My dad...didn't know if he should go back into business.... He owned a lot on the corner and they started digging the basement. So he moved into the Village Hall. We did more business in there than we did when we moved into the new store.

The store was a total loss although some kids came down to look through the ashes. One boy recalled, "I was in second grade. We dug

126   CHANHASSEN: A CENTENNIAL HISTORY

Albert Pauly opened his new store on July 1, 1930.

Albert and his son Fritz stand inside the new store. Notice the sign: Please don't ask for credit on coal.

around the ashes looking for what we thought was skates. It was a flour scoop."

For a time, the Paulys ran their store out of the village hall. A new store went up and opened on July 1, 1930. Viola Buschkowsky said, "They had everything. They even sold gas. They had pumps right out there. They had groceries. They had meats. And they had the Post office in there." Dutch Pauly fondly recalled the store. "My dad had groceries, dry goods, shoes, cognac, farm machinery. My dad would get up at 3:00 in the morning. He would close the store at 11:00 at night. These old codgers, Uncle Nick and my grandfather, they'd play Yuker down on the dry goods counter and he would finally kick them out so he could close up. He had coal too."

Julianne Kerber said, "That store had everything. It had the post office, dry goods, the meat market, the general store. It was the only store in Chanhassen and everybody went there. You got your mail and the gossip was gotten there. There were a couple of old guys that never married that were sitting in these big captain's chairs and they would hear the news and tell the news. We'd go there to find out what was going on."

It had old-fashioned customer service. Gladys Kerber remembered, "People would go into the store and a guy would come up and say 'can I help you?' and then my Dad would say 'I want two cans of corn' so he would go get two cans of corn and then he would say two cans of peas so he would walk right back and get two cans of peas and there was only one kind."

The old Pauly's Store was a busy place. Ed Mason is having his car served. Mary Timmers is at the pump. In the rear, Lorraine Jorissen tends two children: Willard Pauly and Fritz Pauly.

Emil Pauly

The Paulys. Front row: Christine (Lenzen) Pauly, Emil, Henry. Back Row: Albert, Edward, William Pauly

Pauly's Bar

Emil Pauly opened his bar on May 30, 1934. Its construction made a big impression on young Stan Roeser. He recalled, "I remember when they dug the basement for Pauly's Bar. A horse collapsed, fell over from the heat." The bar quickly became a popular spot. Red Jorissen said,

> When liquor came back they built a store for Emil Pauly. Chanhassen was one of the only places for liquor. There was no liquor in Excelsior, Minnetonka, Wayzata, Eden Prairie. Pauly's was a popular place to go. We didn't have music in my day but we had slot machines. They were illegal. People would line up to play them.

Emil Pauly said once, "The population of Chanhassen increased about 300 to 400 on Saturday nights."

But then there were the regulars. Tony Kerber said, "Clarence Geiser and Walter Griepentrog and a couple of those Rasers used to sit in Pauly's in the winter and eat peanuts. Sometimes you couldn't see the floor from the peanut shells. For a quarter you could buy a big pan full of peanuts. Sometimes Dad would go there after church on Sundays. The highlight always at Christmas was to have a Tom and Jerry at Paulys." After mass on Sunday, most of the men retired to Pauly's for, as they called it, the "benediction." Many residents remember stopping by for a Tom and Jerry on Christmas morning.

The Pauly's remodelled the bar in 1966. The building was purchased by the City of Chanhassen as part of the downtown revitalization program and is scheduled to be torn down.

Emil Pauly (right) was an avid fisherman. He is pictured here with Arthur Anderson.

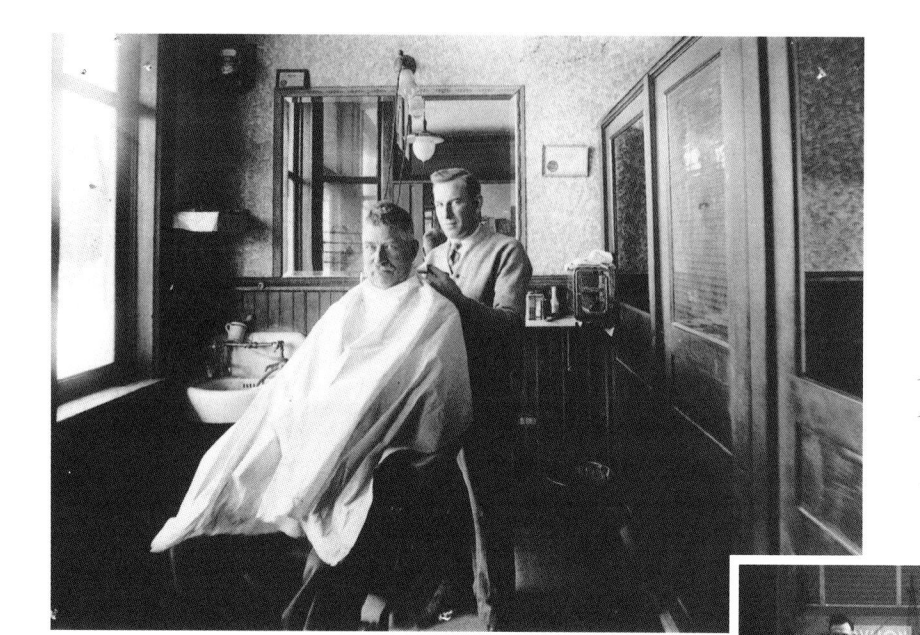

Joe Meuwissen cuts Jacob Jeurissen's hair, circa 1927.

Below: Joe Meuwissen

Joe's Place was the only place in town to get an ice cream cone.

The Pine Grill was built by the Heutmakers after WWII. Next door is Joe's Tavern.

Meuwissens

Joe Meuwissen opened up his store in 1924. He had attended barber school and opened his place as a confectionary (candy store) and barber shop. Red Jorrisen worked at Joe's for several years. He said, "[During the depression] I started working at Joe's. We had a confectionery and soda counter. We had a pool table and he was a barber by trade. So when he wanted to go fishing he would come and get me and I would take care of the place. When he was cutting hair, I would run the soda fountain and sell moonshine alcohol."

Everyone from that period remembered stopping by Joe's for an ice cream cone which featured a double scoop. Tom Kelm explained the secret of Joe's success another way. "My folks were gone quite often so I ate a lot of hamburgers for supper at Joe Meuwissen's," Kelm said. "He had great hamburgers because he never washed the grill in 30 years."

Joe's turtle soup became a legend. His daughetr said, "Once a year he would go out with Johnny Amrhein and Charlie Bird and Klein. They trapped snapping turtles and they cleaned them up and made turtle soup. They put a lot of salt in and sold a lot of beer."

Joe sold the place in 1953. It went through several owners and was renamed "Jerry's Old West." It later became the Pony Express Bar and was torn down in 1995.

The bank was chartered in 1914 and located next to Pauly's Bar. Elmer Kelm (right) took over the cashier's position following his father's death. The Kelm home (below) is still standing on the corner of West 78th Street and Frontier Trail.

State Bank of Chanhassen

The bank was chartered on April 14, 1914 and opened for business on May 4th with capital of $10,000. The staff included Roy Quimby, of Minneapolis, president; Mathew Bongard, vice president; and Henry Kelm, cashier. They built a substantial building next to Pauly's that became popular as the village "theater." In the summer, a large white sheet was hung on the side of the bank and movies were shown.

Henry Kelm, though, died in a year. Elmer Kelm took over his father's position at the bank although he was only seventeen at the time. Elmer was born in 1900 and attended college, a rarity in Chanhassen, graduating from Saint Thomas. He was selected as village treasurer in 1923. Kelm seemed to relish the role of small town banker. Some remember that he gave loans with generous conditions. Dr. Seifert got a loan from the bank after he had been turned down in Excelsior. Seifert became Chanhassen's most popular doctor in town. His office was in Excelsior.

They gave small banks to each new child in town. When they reached an appropriate age, they took the bank down to Mr. Kelm who opened a regular savings account for them. Harold Kerber remembered, "I put my first money there. When I made my First Communion, I had probably $12 and put it in an interest account. When I was 21, I could start spending it." Rita Rojina said, "When you were born you got a bank and they kept the key. You would put in all your pennies and nickels and then when you had enough you took it to the bank and Elmer Kelm opened it and put it in your savings account."

There were hazards to the job. When the bank was robbed in 1931, the thieves took Elmer to Highway 5 and County Road 4 and dumped him. They were caught.

Chanhassen in the 1940s. Joe's Place on the right, then bank.

Politics

In 1928, Kelm stepped into an important political position when he was elected as Carver County Democratic Chairman. The next major election was the fall presidential campaign which pitted Herbert Hoover against Al Smith. Kelm delivered his home town in spectacular fashion. His son, Doug, remembers handing out literature at age six. The Village of Chanhassen voted unanimously for Al Smith, the first Catholic presidential candidate from a major party. the count was seventy to zero. Red Jorrisen remembered, "The minute they counted up the votes, they called WCCO…and the station announced the first votes were coming in from Chanhassen." For a brief moment, it put the quiet town on the national news. In far off Pocatello, Idaho, Richard Lyman was checking on an alfalfa farm. When they posted an election bulletin on the bulletin board, he was surprised to read the name of his hometown among the first returns.

Kelm could not, however, dictate the votes in every election. In fact, the village always marched to its own drummer politcally. In 1924 they have supported Robert LaFollette, the Progressive Party candidate from Wisconsin. In 1932 they matched their unanimity, favoring Roosevelt over Hoover 68 to 0. In 1936 many abandoned Roosevelt. Congressman William Lemke carried the town with a substantial major. Lemke was the hand-picked candidate of Father James Coughlin, the fiery priest whose radio program became a local favorite. Once again, not a single vote for the Republican, Alf Landon. In 1940 the village voted for Wendell Wilkie, probably because Kelm's mentor, Congressman Elmer Ryan, staunchly opposed a third term for Roosevelt. By comparison, the township and the county usually voted Republican.

Truman appointed Kelm to the posts at the Customs Office and the IRS.

Testimonial dinner for Elmer Kelm in 1955. Front row: Karl Rolvaag, Loretta and Elmer Kelm, Muriel and Hubert Humphrey. The two men in the rear are unidentified.

Kelm was known for the ham radio set that he kept in his basement.

Kelm transformed Minnesota politics during the 1940s after he was chosen state chairman. In 1940 he chosen state Democratic Chairman. It was one of the most powerful posts in the state. Typically, appointments were decided by the congressional delegation. After a sweeping defeat, it left all patronage in the hands of Elmer Kelm. His son remembered, "All postmasters, rural carriers, defense jobs were all patronage. Our house was a revolving door."

In those days, the rivalry between the Farmer–Labor Party and the regular Democratic Party split the liberal vote and handed dominance to the Republican Party. Harold Stassen had burst on the scene and swept away the opposition.

Kelm was summoned to a meeting with President Roosevelt in the White House. Roosevelt told him, "I'm running again in 1944. It could be a close election and I've got to have a unified party." With the help of a dynamic young politician named Hubert Humphrey, Kelm negotiated a merger of the two groups into a single Democratic–Farmer–Labor Party. He made Humphrey the state chairman for Roosevelt to give him statewide exposure.

Elmer Benson, the most popular FL leader, dragged his feet, believing that Kelm was too conservative to head the new party. He said, "Kelm is a fascist. So is Humphrey. This is absolutely no good but we must unite." In 1944 Kelm became the first DFL chairman. In those days, party leaders wielded tremendous influence dispensing patronage jobs.

Kelm received his own reward with an appointment as state collector of internal revenue. He sold the banking interest in 1950 to Frank Schneider. In 1952, he became collector of customs after the IRS moved to civil service regulations. After Eisenhower won the 1952 election, Kelm resigned. The Kelms had one of the first telephones in town and some neighbors remember dropping by to use it. He is fondly remembered as a ham radio operator. "He had a little radio studio. He used to talk on the radio which we thought was just a really big deal. Sometimes he would interfere with some of the radio programs." With the handle of "Kelly" he spent hours on the air with W0JDO. "The only place in Minnesota with a cemetery in the loop." He died in 1957, a day after Hubert Humphrey had visited his bedside. In 1968 Hubert Humphrey gave his first campaign speech after his nomination to a Minnesota audience. He told them, "If it hadn't been for a small town banker from Chanhassen, I would never have had a chance. He gave me the opportunity."

Ray Rettler manned the D-X Station.

D–X

The Minnesota Victoria Oil Company opened a new D-X station across the street from Joe's Bar just before World War II. At the grand opening, music was provided by the Victoria Concert Band. One band member, Charles Schneider, remembered that the band moved into the bars, instruments and all, after the concert and kept playing through the evening, mostly in tune. Finally, Chanhassen had a full-fledged gas station.

Stan Roeser remembered Ray Rettler fondly. He said,

> It was almost like a boy's club. He was an easy going guy who didn't take his business too seriously. He was endlessly promoting baseball games, football games, and boxing matches. That's where the kids hung out. There was a vacant lot across the street and we used to go play football and Ray would be over and play. When a car would come up and ring the buzzer he'd have to dart across the street and sometimes not very promptly because he felt more like playing football.

Mause "Mouse" Kerber in the Chanhassen Garage, 1930s.

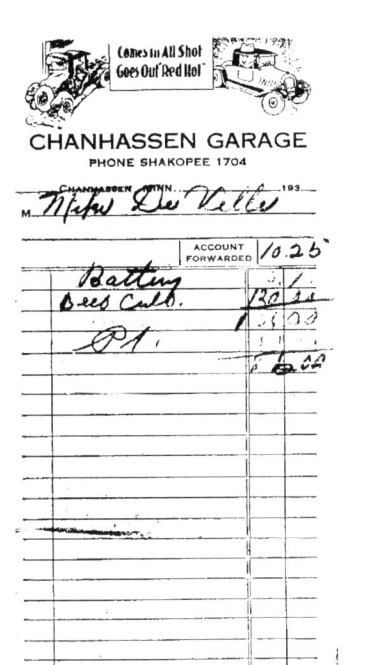

Feed Mill

Hank Schutrop owned the feed mill. Ron Roeser remembered, "They were good workers. All the farmers dealt with him."

Ole Kerber's Farm

Most of the town's people got their milk from Ole and Mary Kerber. Bob Meuwissen recalled, "That's where we got our milk every night. Everybody would go up and fill your milk bottles." It also gave Chanhassen its peculiar ambiance. Rita Meuwissen said, "His cows would go down main street. About 4:15 the cows would all be waiting in the pasture and you would come and help take them down main street. When the cows went potty, nobody cleaned it up."

Below: Susan Meuwissen behind Joe's Place. Next door is Ole Kerber's house.

John and Elizabeth (Schlenk) Rettler in the fall of 1953. Photograph is taken in front of their home. It is now the site of the Colonial Center.

Elmer Kelm lived in this house for most of the 1920s. It was located where the feed mill was and orginally owned by Gerhard Schroeder, first president of the city council.

Armistice Day Snowstorm

In Minnesota, the weather makes its own news. On Armistice Day 1940, a big snow storm hit town. Henry Dimler said, "We pulled cars out of the snow banks on Hwy 212 for four days. That was the worst storm. I've never seen anything like it." Dutch Pauly recalled, "Schlefsky, my plumber, left early and got as far as Heck's Hill. It took three weeks before they got the car unstuck."

On the farms, they were stuck in their homes. Julianne Kerber said, "They made ropes from the house to the barn so they could hang on to a string. We had pudding and more pudding. We had milk, milk and more milk or it would have been spoiled."

Larry Klein remembered that when the township asked for help in re-opening Hwy 101, the state wanted to permanently take over maintenance. He and his father were at Pauly's store when he overheard a couple township board members meeting with a representative of the state.

World War II

Every year the women of Saint Hubert's Church held a "Sisters' Shower." They would pick up small gifts for the nuns and bring food that they could use during the winter. Ron Roeser remembered when his mother came home from the shower on December 7, 1941. He said, "I remember my mother coming home from that party and saying that they had just heard the news. Somehow through the Kelms, we learned that Pearl Harbor had been bombed. I couldn't eat I was so scared. I just had this idea that the Japanese were only on the other side of the woods. Then the war turned into a great time for me because of all the things you could imagine, war games we played and pretending." Stan Roeser said, "I could see the Japs descending on

California. That was the first time I ever heard my father use a swear word. He said, "Those sons of bitches. They're going to pay."

Many of the young men enlisted or were drafted. Some stayed because they received farm exemptions. Henry Wrase said, "I was exempt from going into the service. But I met all my buddies that were going in on the bus when the day came that they were shipped out. One fellow said, 'Henry, you stay home and make sure that we've got enough food.' That was the thing that a farmer had to do. We had to plow every acre of land that was available to produce the corn or milk."

Rita Meuwissen organized the home front. She was working at Pauly's store at the time and kept a photo display in the front window at Pauly's. With Clarice Coulter, she started the *Chan News*, a monthly newsletter about the boys in the service.

> Guido Kerber left for the Army and is stationed in California.
> Mercil Bongard has been promoted to the office of Sergeant.
> Claude Sinnen has been sent overseas but we do not know where.
> Douglas Kelm was home on furlough.
> Bill Hullsiek …has been in the Hawaiian Islands.
> Harry Pauly…has finished his boot training at the Great Lakes.
> Dutch Pauly was home in July and is now at Camp Lewis, Washington.
> Rudolph Graftland was sent to California where his wife joined him.
> Martin Schlenk…is somewhere in the South Pacific.
> Mrs. John Cash (Beatrice Rettler) received a telegram from her husband. He had been over in India.
> Walter Hansen arrived home Sunday morning from deep in the heart of Texas.
> Billy Kirtz was home on a three day furlough.

It was Chanhassen's first newspaper, but then not much else happened. "Who said Chanhassen isn't up to date?" she wrote. "Main Street was tarred by the highway department last week." For local stories, Rita noted that the *Times Tribune* paper route was being passed from Tommy Kelm to Delores Melchior. This, of course, was big news. The Roeser kids had control over the *Star Journal* route. Her sharpest comments were for a trio of boys. She reported, "Stanley Roeser, Tommy Kelm, and Bobby Meuwissen took a bus to Minneapolis last week to see a ball game. There must have been something special in the deal because they wouldn't take Rita."

Everyone faced rationing. Edna Wrase said, "During the war, you had to have stamps for food. Everything was hard to get." Henry said, "You had to have stamps for gas. You were allotted so many stamps for your car and if you had tractors and things, you got what you really

Rita Meuwissen placed photographs of Chanhassen soldiers in Pauly's window during WWII.

needed." Rita Meuwissen remembered working at Pauly's Store. She said, "Stuff was rationed. The corn flakes and stuff faded so we'd turn them around on the shelf and put the good side to the front. Albert found some cleanser down in the basement that had to be sold because it had been standing there too long. I put two cans of cleanser with a package of raisins and said limit one. People came back three, four times in one day to get those raisins." To kids, its meant no ice cream, no candy bars.

The *Chan News* carried a poem from one of the village's young men.

CHANHASSEN
By CPL. Joseph Marschall

Cpl. Joe Marschall, in his leisure moments in the territory of Hawaii, composed and dedicated the following poem in honor of his home town of Chanhassen and the people who live there:

I'm sitting here and thinking
Of a place so far away,
The place I'm coming back to,
It's where I plan to stay.

It's not a town or city
It's really not so big.
But what's an oak before it grows
Nothing but a twig!

The place that I am thinking of
Is a village small and fair;
Everything I held so dear,
Is waiting for me there.

It's not the town where I was born,
But it's where I spent my youth,
Where I realized my first ambition,
To wear a three-piece long pants suit,

It's where I spent my school days,
Where I first learned of puppy love,
Where I listened to the pastor
Tell of Him who's up above!

It will always bring back memories,
Of vacations from our school,
Of the times we swam together
In that big Lake Susan pool.

Cpl. Joseph Marschall

Of the hunting and the fishing
Near this earthly paradise,
The coolness of the water
And the blueness of the skies.

In my dreams again I see it,
Even Albert Pauly's Store
On the corner where it now stands,
And the place it was before,

I can hear the ringing church bells,
Calling all good folks together,
Coming from the farms and village,
Regardless of the weather.

This village is Chanhassen
Its had its joys, and sorrows too,
Of it I'll keep on thinking,
Also of you and you and you!

Willard Bongard, Mrs. Kerber, and Guido Kerber leaving for the service in the fall of 1944.

Yes it's a fine compliment to the little village of Chanhassen and its fine citizens. Cpl. Marschall sends season's greetings to all his friends, and wishes to thank many of them for sending him Christmas, packages that arrived at his destination a short time ago.

Stan Roeser remembered the VE Day. He said,

At the end of the war it was typical Chanhassen. Everybody went to church to say prayers. The edict came that all bars were to close but the back door at Pauly's was open and everybody went from church into the back door of Pauly's. The place was filled. It was a tough time and people were glad it was over.

The veterans returned to the "village small and fair" having seen the world. But Chanhassen had barely changed. Doug Kelm remembered, "There was no attorney in town, no doctor, no dentist, no CPA. There wasn't a constable other than on paper." Tom Klingelhutz said that at the end of the war, "The City of Chanhassen had a flag with forty-seven stars on it and a map in the village hall depicting Oklahoma as Indian Territory." Things would begin changing.

Chapter Eight
Rituals

O<small>N THE SURFACE</small> it might appear that nothing ever happened in Chanhassen. But it only lacked the events that cause headlines. In fact, there was rarely a dull moment in the village. Much of that activity took place around Saint Hubert's Church and School. As Stan Roeser put it, "There was no such thing as separation of church and state. Everyone in the community was Catholic, except the mayor and the property of the church and the property of the village was pretty much interchangeable and nobody had any real qualms about it." When asked how the village and the church got along with each other, Al Sinnen said, "They got along real good because they were one and the same."

Saint Hubert's Church and School

Daily life was ruled by the school schedule and the calendar of holy days.

Every Sunday morning, you were expected at church. Harold Kerber wrote: "There were two masses on Sundays—one mass had a German sermon and the other mass had an English sermon. The children sat in the front pews—girls on the left side and the boys on the right side. A few years later this was changed. That is when pew rent started. One Sunday during the year, you could rent a pew or more. They ranged in price from about $8 a year for a pew in the rear to $4 a year for the front pews."

After mass you had only a little free time until kids gathered for instructions. "As we were growing up and in grade school," Kerber said, "every Sunday during school months we would have to get instructions, plus Vespers and Benediction to the upper grades. During Lent it was Stations of the Cross every Friday and Sunday afternoon plus instructions."

School days started early. One former student remembered, "We walked across fields to school, about 1½ miles in time for the 8 am Mass on school days which were Monday, Tuesday, Wednesday, Friday, and Saturday. Thursday was the free day, not Saturday."

The school building was one of the important landmarks in Chanhassen. There were three classrooms after the 1920s: first through third, fourth through sixth, and seventh and eighth in the "big

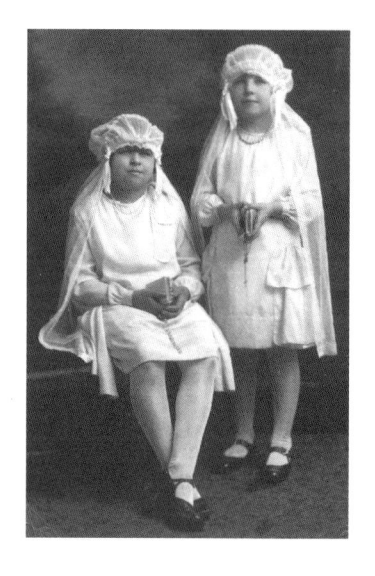

First Communion was a big day for the children of Chanhassen. Top: Charlotte and Rosemary Pauly in the 1920s. Below: Donald and Kenneth Pauly.

Saint Hubert's School and Convent circa 1940.

room." The nuns lived upstairs. Outside, they kept a garden behind the school. There was a large shed where wood and coal were stored to heat the classrooms and the nun's living quarters. To the north stood the church woods. Henry Dimler recalled, "The church woods was the site of the horse barn which would hold about twenty horses for the parishioners. We kids used to play there."

The nuns who taught at Saint Hubert's are recalled with generally fond memories. Rosemary Pauly Mingo said,

> Sister Ruth Mary taught 4th, 5th, and 6th grade. She was really strict. She could reprimand those boys and the girls too. For 1st, 2nd, and 3rd grade we had Sister Bernadette. She was about seventeen when she became a nun. Chanhassen was her first parish and mother and dad had her for a teacher. She taught the girl's embroidery and different sewing methods. She did that outside the classroom. She was an awfully sweet person. Sister Phormina raised chickens and she was one of the cooks. She was just an all around worker. She'd make things like dolls out of crepe paper. Then she'd decorate them. If anyone would bring her a bushel of corn or something for her chickens, she'd give them one. So of course I did that. I was in heaven. Sister Elfrida took care of the church altar cloths and decorated the church. They used to teach piano. Another time, Sister Josephine was a tap dancer. She taught us tap dancing.

144   CHANHASSEN: A CENTENNIAL HISTORY

Our School Days

Above: 1924 1st row: (l-r) Donald Trutnau, Lawrence Mason, Gilbert Kurvers, Ray Schutrop, ?, ? Baker, Kenneth Pauly, Donald Kurvers, Harold Kerber. 2nd row: Catherine Schutrop, Vernice Niedenfier, Florence Klingelhutz, Florence Klein, Helen Welter, Myrtle Jorissen, Genevive Jacques, Mildred Welter, ?, Laura Klein. 3rd row: August Welter, Marion Mason, Lorraine Kurvers, Ethel Kurvers, Marcella Rein, Luverna Fischer, Rosella Klingelhutz, Florence Mason, Angela Kerber, Urban Kerber. 4th row: ?, Ray Rettler, Willard Pauly, Victor Schmieg, Clarence Schmieg, Edwin Kerber, Wilfred Kerber, ? Baker, Harold Roeser, Wilfred Fischer.

Opposite page, lower photograph: 1938 Front row: (l-r) Stan Rojina, Fred Kurtz, Lawrence Klein, Bernard Bongard, LeRoy Wellens, Charles Bird, Pat Kerber, Eugene Miller, Bob Meuwissen, Stan Roeser, Bob Kerber, Harold Welter, Art Mason, Tom Kelm, Ray Melchior, Don Schumacher. 2nd row: Dave Kerber, Alvin Jeurissen, Roger Bongard, Paul Rojina, Gordon Wellens, Walter Kerber, Ed Jeurissen, Gilbert Kerber, Jerome Kerber, George Kerber, Steve Klein, Harold Miller, Roman Sinnen, Don Schumacher. 3rd row: Gladys Kerber, Loretta Kerber, JoAnn Miller, LaVern Buschkowsky, Rita Meuwissen, Bernice Benhagen, Celine Kerber, Laura Mae Kerber, Doris Kerber, Dorothy Jeurissen, Janice Welter, Rosella Schroeder, Jeanette Bongard, Evelyn Schroeder, Dorothy Bongard, Collette Sinnen, Mary Klein, Judy Kerber, Alice Kerber. 4th row: Francis Klein, Bill Kurtz, Dorothy Wellens, Frances Rojina, Elvira Kerber, Alfreda Welter, Irene Sinnen, Georgina Wellens, Viola Klein, Myra Klingelhutz, Dorothy Klein, Rich Schumacher, fred Zimmer, Arnold Schroeder, Norbert Welter. Back row: Kathleen Kerber, Dorothy Klingelhutz, Luella Klingelhutz, Rosemary Kurvers, Bernice Klingelhutz, Marie Kurtz, Jim Kerber, Florian Kerber, Edward Klein, Al Sinnen, Kenneth Kerber, Willard Bongard, Guido Kerber, Willis Klein, Harry Pauly, Fred Miller.

Above: 1931. 1st row, left to right: Willard Bongard, Guido Kerber, Edwin Klein, ?, Dorothy Wellens, ?, Germaine Jacques, Luella Klingelhutz, Rosemary Kurvers, Irene Sinnen, Dorothy Klingelhutz, Bernice Klingelhutz, Kathleen Kerber, Frances Rojina, Marie Kurtz, Elfreda Welter, ?, Peggy Kerber. 2nd row: ?, Roman Wellens, ?, Florian Kerber, Jim Kerber, Rosemary Pauly, Douglas Kelm, Wendel Trutnau, Vernon Kerber, Jim Welter Willis Klein, Lawrance Schutrop, Joe Klein, Leander Kerber. 3rd row: Marion Mason, Henrietta Kelm, Charoltte Pauly, Viola Buschkowsky, Esther Welter, Claude Sinnen, Clarice Pauly, Rolendis Kerber, Alphonse Lalak, Aldine Miller, Bernie Welter, Evelyn Klingelhutz, Fred Bongard, ?, Lawrence Jacques, Sylvester Jacques, Lucille Kerber, ? Kurtz, Mercel Bongard, Laverna Bongard, ?. 4th row: Angela Kerber, Mildred Welter, Florence Klingelhutz, Luverna Fischer, Catherine Schutrop, Rosella Rettler, Marcella Kerber, Reuben Bongard, Wilfred Fischer, Elmo Schmitt, Ray Rettler, Bernie Kerber, Don Trutnau, Urban Kerber, ?, Donald Pauly, Harold Kerber, Fr. Florentine Kurzer, OFM.

Stan Roeser probably put it best when he defined the mystery of the nun's world, saying, "The nuns were kind of an unusual world. Almost like there was a veil between their teaching lives and their private lives. You hardly ever entered their living area. They had their own eating place and their own chapel. The few times that I got in there it was almost like you were in another world."

All the students remembered that part of their school day was taken up with chores. Clarice Pauly Coulter remembered, "We not only had school but we did a lot of work like in the fall of the year we piled wood and cleaned houses. Everybody worked together."

The rooms had big pot-bellied stoves that required a constant supply of firewood. Tony Kerber said, "In the northwest corner of the room we had a big pot bellied stove and I would sit four feet away from that stove. Then sister would say, 'Tony, it's getting cool in here, better put a chunk of wood in.' The boys usually carried the wood and carried out the ashes." Henry Dimler recalled,

The boys were expected to clean the nuns' chicken coop when asked.

> After the farm work had been finished, the farmers would come to the church to cut the wood for the church and school stoves. In late November they would haul the wood up to the school. They would use big saws to cut the wood to size. I remember a steam engine used to power the saws. We had a wagon, a long wagon with high iron wheels. We kids would help load the wagons. Several of the boys would pull from the front pole of the wagon and two or three boys would push from behind. We didn't get much school work done for about a week.

Dimler remembered Father Florence walking behind the boys, smiling, and prodding them along with the rope belt of his Franciscan habit.

Boys got to feed the nuns' chickens and clean the coop, usually on Fridays. Tony Kerber said, "In the shed there was room for about one hundred chickens which provided eggs and meat for the nuns. Every spring they bought chicks. The nuns would beg for chicken feed and straw from the farm children. Drinking water was in a crock cooler filled each morning with a pail filled from a hand pump cistern. In the winter months, it had to be emptied each day after school as it would freeze solid."

But the girls had their tasks. Gladys Kerber recalled, "We had outhouses and usually the 7th and 8th grade girls had to scrub them." Clarice Pauly Coulter recalled one day when she and her friends were playing up by the cemetery on a day off. "Sister Phormina came out of

Sister Carlinda taught at St. Hubert's School

the convent and hollered at us to come and do some work. Myrt [Myrtl Jorissen] says, 'duck,' so we fell to the ground and we didn't go and help her. So when we got to school on Monday we had to write a penance about one hundred times. And if that wasn't enough when we got home we caught more hell."

What most remember is that parents, nuns and priests, and townspeople—all the adults—raised them. Indeed, in Chanhassen's case, it took a village to raise the child.

Tom Klingelhutz said, "I remember one time raising a little hell in school and the nun sent a note home to my mother and as I was crossing the creek I pulled the note out and threw it in the creek. That wasn't so bad because no one knew about it until next Sunday. After mass the nun and my mother got to talking and they found out I didn't bring the note home and I really caught hell."

Doug Kelm, looking back on his childhood, said,

> We live today in a world where things move fast and change so often. In first grade, my father was taught by a nun, Sister Bernadette. Many years later…I was taught by her. When one got into trouble as a child it didn't take long for discipline to occur because Joe [Meuwissen] would call up Elmer or visit Elmer over a beer and say your son Doug has been doing such and such this afternoon and that would result in severe discipline when Elmer came home. I lived in this atmosphere not in fear but in knowing that I had a lot of uncles all over town who kept an eye on things and maybe were not faraid to…tell your parents if you misbehaved.

After graduation, some students went to Guardian Angels School in Chaska. Others attended Eden Prairie High School. Most youths stopped their formal education after high school.

Easter

As Ron Roeser remembered, "Holy week was a big deal…"

> For boys that served mass …you would have Holy Thursday which was a long session in church and then Good Friday was another long session, including all day and then on Saturday you had to be there at five or four in the morning and there were these long readings and everything was done in Latin. So you would get up at five and the priest would light the Easter fire. Eventually they got smart and used lighter fluid. It got to be such a long day and everything had to be down pat.

Tom Kelm remembered the bells of Saint Hubert's.

> At Easter time, my mother felt that every time the church bells rang we were supposed to go. I can remember on Holy Thursday, I served mass, and then they'd have an hour for mass servers that you had to put in, then you had to put your hour in with your family and then end up going back at 8 pm for services.

The bells were special to Ron Roeser, too. He said,

> On Holy Thursday they would ring all the bells in the church. Any bell that they had would be rung and from then until Saturday there would be no bells in the church. They would use this wooden thing called a clapper which had a real desolate sound. The bells, I actually believed that the bells were gone and they would come back at the gloria on Holy Saturday at noon when lent ended and at that time everything would be rung.
>
> It was at that time the first Easter eggs would appear. My grandfather would sit there waiting for his lunch on Holy Saturday to hear the bells ring so he could have his noon sausage. 'Come on,' he'd say, 'ring those bells!'

Corpus Christi Day

In early May the town celebrated Corpus Christi Day in a grand manner. "That was our biggest holiday," said Lorraine Roeser. Preparations began several days before the event. Families placed chapels around the church woods for the big day. These small houses were only shacks, called holy houses, but they took great pride in decorating and had a bit of holy competition. "We were involved in decorating one of the chapels," said Rosemary Pauly Mingo. "That was always a big weekend when we'd go to Aunt Margaret's. She would have baked a lot of things. We'd walk in her house and smell all these

Corpus Christi procession.

Corpus Christi Day was one of the biggest events of the year. A parade, led by school children dressed in white, marched to three stations located near St. Hubert's Church.

bakery goods because we always did it on the Saturday before. My aunt would come out from Saint Paul with her husband and he did all the electrical stuff. Putting the electric lights in and an electric cross lit up." Those Christmas lights are still talked about among the village residents.

On the Sunday morning of Corpus Christi Day, the whole congregation marched from chapel to chapel in a grand procession. Rosemary Mingo remembered, "We girls would carry baskets with flower petals and the day before we'd get all that ready. That was a big day. Then the Mother's Society would pray the rosary while we were walking. The church bells rang and it was so magnificent! The acolytes carried those swinging lamps and a canopy over the priest and he carried this big monstrance."

Doug Kelm recalled,

> It was really a great thing. After mass the entire parish would leave the church and parade down Saint Hubert's Street to the east with little girls carrying baskets of flower petals that they would distribute and boys carrying banners and incense and large candle holders and the like. As they marched the bells would be ringing…in the steeple of Saint Hubert's. Just to the east of the school was a little chapel and we stopped there to have a brief benediction during which time the bells would stop the ringing and the choir would sing and then we would move on again with the bells ringing to still another chapel. As I recall there were four of them scattered in what was called the church woods.

Ron Roeser summed up the spirit of the day, saying, "The whole street was covered with petals. It seemed kind of foreign."

Doug Kelm remembered that the boys looked forward to the job of bell-ringer.

> One of the jobs that had the greatest stature for the boys was to go up into the steeple because the smaller bells would have the habit of turning over completely...and the young boys would turn the bell back. I remember the time when Willis Klein...bent over to take the bell by the rim to turn it back over just as the large bell came swinging along. It caught him in the buttocks and sent him riding over the smaller bell he was about to turn over.

The Chicken Dinner

The Harvest Festival Chicken Dinner, held every August, was the biggest day of the year in Chanhassen. In the midst of the Depression, the congregation needed money and started the dinners in 1934. They dug a basement under the church using hand shovels, wheel barrows and horse-power. Dutch Pauly remembered that a work crew initially began to dig out a hole for a new furnace. He said, "We weren't going to go under the sanctuary. So Fritz (his brother) started digging it out [and] that was the kitchen. We had one chicken dinner there and we decided to dig under the sacristy and the priest's quarters to make a big kitchen. So we got all that done." The dinner proved to be a great success, serving more than one thousand dinners each year.

For a quiet rural town, it gave a break to the dog days of summer. Stan Roeser said, "I can recall the excitement started to mount already, a month or so before when a banner was usually erected across main street advertising the event. Even the day before the chicken dinner was a memorable time." The women of the parish all picked up their chickens and the scent of roasting chickens wafted over the village on Saturday night. His brother, Ron, recalled, "You knew it was getting close because all the farmers would come into town and build these wooden stands for the bingo and the beer stands. The back part of Village Hall was the dart stand."

Stan Roeser wrote: "The farm kids would all be in for the day with their parents. The women would work in the church basement getting ready for the big meal—a couple of thousand or more were usually served—while overall clad men would be bustling about the village park all day erecting canvasses and setting up stands."

Cooking the Chicken dinner, 1959.

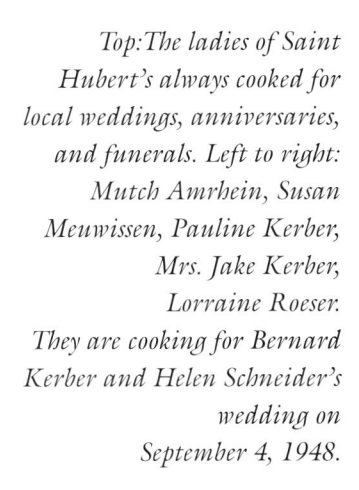

Top: The ladies of Saint Hubert's always cooked for local weddings, anniversaries, and funerals. Left to right: Mutch Amrhein, Susan Meuwissen, Pauline Kerber, Mrs. Jake Kerber, Lorraine Roeser. They are cooking for Bernard Kerber and Helen Schneider's wedding on September 4, 1948.

The boys loved to set up boxing matches on that day. Stan Roeser wrote,

> As the various stands were set up someone would usually bring out a set of boxing gloves—the various stands bore some resemblance to a ring. There were some subtleties involved in this boxing business. Trick was to get yourself matched against someone you knew you could at least hold your own with while never really admitting you might be afraid of slugging it out with a really tough kid.
>
> This was long before the equal rights amendment era, but there was little sex discrimination. I remember my sister Mary— "mare" we called her, was a just plain tough kid despite the fact she was a girl. She got in the ring with a boy and they were flailing away at each other with gusto when "mare", who was getting the worst of it, suddenly burst out bawling, ending the match.

On the big day, everything started at eleven in the morning. The food, of course, was the main attraction. Stan Roeser said, "The dinner—well, it was what you'd call a gourmet meal today—chicken, mashed potatoes, gravy, dressing and all—nothing I've tasted before or since was quite like it for some reason. Much of what went into it was donated from the gardens of parishioners."

Roeser remembered that Elmer Kelm handled the PA system. "The town banker handled the microphone. He was a ham radio operator too, and had sort of a mellifluous voice-probably would have made a great radio announcer. His familiar voice calling 'number up to 299 now line up to eat' seems to be indelibly etched in my memory as I recall Chanhassen's chicken dinner."

It fell to the women of Saint Hubert's to prepare more than one thousand chicken dinners. Rita Meuwissen Rojina remembered her first year,

> I was put on gravy with Louise Thompson. We got down in the basement and here the two older women didn't show up to make gravy. We both looked at each other and here we are both pregnant and Mutch [Amrhein] yelled, "Get that gravy going!" What do you do? "There's the kerosene stove, put some juice on it, get it hot, mix some flour and throw it in!" So we did. We'd look at each other and we'd taste it and we made gravy and I'm still making the gravy. We would go on Saturday and brown all this chicken and after the first year we got the hang of it.

It was the ultimate test of a woman's skill in a society that treasured good food. Stan Roeser said,

> My mother liked to complain occasionally about the work, but the pull of all the horses in Carver County—and that would have been quite a lot of horsepower in those years—couldn't have kept her away. The close association with the other women of the parish and reports on who "really worked" and who just stood around and pretended to be "busy," provided enough gossip fodder to last well into the winter.

For kids, it was a magical time, free from responsibility with plenty to do. A band played polka music in the bandstand. Later the group might be "Pearl and Ade," a popular couple of the 1940s heard regularly over WCCO.

The beer stand made lots of money. Stan Roeser wrote, "The beer stand, incidentally, did a bountiful business all day, from about 11 in the morning till about 11 at night. Tap beer was served up in endless rounds of glasses. The beer trucks—Hamm's, Schmidt's, Grain Belt—would back right up to the grounds, and 16 or 18 full barrels would be consumed through the day, yet I don't recall any drunken scenes or serious mishaps ever marring this event." One person said that most kids probably had their first beer at the chicken dinner when they were fourteen or fifteen years old.

The men of the parish kept busy running the bingo game and the contests. Stan Roeser said,

> In the village park there was the candy store, the card game stand, the dart game, the beer stand, of course, amid a bingo stand the size of which I've never seen matched. I can still hear the pleasant drone of the bingo numbers being called off—recall the gripping excitement when you got one number away from a

Kids got to ride the Northland Dairy Wagon during the 1959 Chicken Dinner. This is an unusual view of the village from the north. The white house on the left belonged to Jack Rettler. The feed mill looms to the right.

bingo—the command to "hold your cards" while a winning card was being checked.

The whole event wound up with the prize drawing. Twenty prizes or so in books of raffle tickets were distributed to every family in the parish. You either bought 'em or tried to sell 'em. The prizes—well, there were items like a case of motor oil, or $5 in cash, or a grease job from the filling station, or a quilt-pretty minor stuff, but win one of them and you felt like a king.

Christmas

The year drew a close at Christmas. For Julianne Kerber, the season started with the sausage.

> We usually had meat at Christmas time. It wouldn't be Christmas unless we had blood sausage. All that got done in the house and it was really a chore on the wood stove. Us kids would come home from school and the walls were literally covered from the steam and the stove and the cold weather. I think they just dripped with grease. We hated it yet we looked forward to it because our Grandmother Kerber would be there helping.

The first snowfall of the season usually came before the Yuletide and brought its usual delights. Children dusted off their sleds and headed outdoors. One former youth said, "The best sledding was on Brose's Hill on what they call North Lotus Lake Park. We used to go down on Frontier Trail at night. On a moonlit night we used to take a lantern and set it in the corner. If a car came up they would know we were sliding down. We would spend whole days down there."

Following traditional German custom, the tree went up on Christmas Eve. Clarice Pauly wrote, "They didn't set up ahead of time. That was done after we all went to bed and I would go in by the boys. The three of us would be in bed together and hear the noise. When we would get up in the morning there would be a tree and all our toys."

On Christmas morning, everyone headed to Saint Hubert's for mass. Lorraine Roeser knew it was Christmas when she heard the sleigh bells. She said, "The farmers came with horses and the barns were right in front of our house. You could hear those bells ringing." Clarice Pauly recalled, "We went to 5:00 am mass and then over to the liquor store for cheer. I followed the crowd. When [the Martin] Schlenks lived across the street we went to midnight mass then Schlenks would have us over and we would make sausage and stuff."

Gladys Kerber remembered,

> On Christmas Eve day you worked hard and went to bed early so Santa Claus would come and then you would get up early because we had to be at church at five in the morning. I know there were a few times when the weather was bad my dad would bring us to church with the horses. I still like Christmas mass when it is dark. I just got used to going out in the dark and then with six brothers, there were always two that had to serve mass and the church things were all different than now.
>
> For breakfast we had blood sausage. We made our own blood and liver sausage. We made popcorn balls and we got the apple, banana, and orange and then we always had fruitcake. When we got older my Dad would go to what they called a poultry raffle. A couple of times he won a live turkey. I remember when we had our first turkey. It was a real treat.

Finally, the Christmas presents. Clarice Pauly said, "We didn't get a lot of toys. We might get a sled or something. The tree...had candles on it and one night we would light all the candles and sit there and watch it. People thought that because we had a store we would get toys and have all the ice cream and candy that we wanted but it wasn't that way." Although there were not many gifts, they were still treasures. Tom Klingelhutz recalled, "When I was young my sisters were pretty good to me. My sister Sally used to give me silver dollars that I still have to this day. My sister Evelyn and Marie sent me an erector set when I was in grade school. When I was seven, we were sitting in the living room and all at once I saw a light in the kitchen going around and around and here was an electric train set up on the kitchen table and I still have that up in my attic.

Stanford Fennelle painted this Chanhassen scene as part of a Works Project Administration grant in 1939. It shows an unusual view of town facing St. Hubert's from the east. From the collections of the Minnesota Historical Society.

If the structure of Chanhassen society—the annual calendar of events, the close watch of the nuns and townspeople, the lack of stores—seems restrictive to us today, it is not remembered like that. "What I remember best is the freedom," Ron Roeser said. Another longtime resident said, "During my childhood I enjoyed the freedom of open fields and wooded areas. The freedom of being carefree, without a worry in the world."

Chapter Nine
Shakers and Movers

THE CARVER COUNTY CENTENNIAL HISTORY BOOK described the town in the mid-fifties in simple terms. It read: "Chanhassen has an approximate population of two hundred. The village has no active fire department. Saint Hubert's Catholic School is the only school in the town. The town boasts one elevator, one bank, one general and grocery store, one garage, and two taverns." A *Minneapolis Star* article from the mid-sixties echoed the historian's view, saying, "For decades the hamlet of Chanhassen dozed in obscurity, devoted to the virtues of standing still." But these observations missed an important shift in the leadership of the village.

At the end of World War II, the soldiers came home to Chanhassen. They had seen other parts of the world. More importantly they had learned to work as part of a large team. As those veterans replaced the older leaders of the village, Chanhassen no longer stood still. Reuben Bongard came back from the Navy and opened an implement store in 1947. Across the street, Val and Lou Heutmaker built the Pine Grill between the bank and Joe's. The Schutrops had already built a towering elevator for the feed mill in 1945.

Gene Coulter returned from a stint in the Army. He had come to the village after his marriage to Clarice Pauly. She remembered, "I met

Gene Coulter. This photograph was taken in 1939 behind Elmer Kelm's house.

The Village of Chanhassen, circa 1950. Notice that the Pine Grill now fills the space between Joe's and the bank.

Chanhassen in the late 1940s. Three big changes took place. Rueben Bongard opened an implement store. The Feed Mill built its tall stack. Finally, the Redbirds had a baseball field just north of the church.

Gene through Jack Herber. They worked together in Minneapolis at Johnson's Refrigeration. My dad's refrigerator at the house went out one night and he called Johnson's and they sent Jack out and Jack said there's this nice fellow you should meet."

Coulter was born in East Grand Forks and came to the Twin Cities to attend the Dunwoody Institute where he learned refrigeration. He got drafted in 1941. After the war, he and two friends started their own successful refrigeration parts business. He quickly became involved in community affairs and helped organize the American Legion post. Harold Kerber remembered, "He was smart, a good talker. Some people did not like him because he went forward too fast." He kept up the pace for almost thirty years.

The Red Birds

Reuben Bongard had a dream. He wanted a baseball team for his town. Baseball was meant for Chanhassen. It was a game played in fields in the summer whose progress was measured in innings and not minutes. The sport had always been a popular pastime. One former player said, "He wasn't flashy but he got things done."

Bongard had a right-hand man in Ollie Iverson, who became the assistant coach. Iverson was a veteran who had landed at Normandy Beach on D-Day. He was in his forties and ran a barber shop in Glen Lake. Ron Roeser recalled, "Ole was kind of our hero. He could throw the knuckle ball. He was a funny, wild Norwegian. Everybody looked up to him. He was Rueben's right hand man. He could still pitch when he was in his 60s. We loved him for batting practice. He could throw them right down the pipe."

In 1947 Bongard organized the Chanhassen Red Birds. First they needed a field. Bongard drafted Roeser, Bob Meuwissen, Tom Kelm and others to clear the land north of the church. Tom Kelm remembered, "We cut 300 trees by hand and then we blew up the stumps. Dutch was lucky that it didn't hit the stained glass windows [at his store]. It just hit the basement windows. Stumps flying through the air!" Stan Roeser recalled, "I remember stepping off the bus one afternoon coming home from high school and that whole area was bulldozed down, woods and all."

The county lent a hand. Although many players remembered that Bongard had persuaded the commissioners to act, Tom Kelm believed that it was his father's political connections that won the day.

> [Elmer Kelm] went over to the Carver County Commissioners and asked if they'd do him a favor. We had to get some equipment in there and level it. They said, "We'll have Ferris swing by and level that whole thing for you." The county auditor, Schimelpfenig, starting objecting to it, it was church property. Dad called in the county attorney, John Fahey. John said, 'Yeah, yeah. It's perfectly legal,' and closed the book.
>
> After it was leveled we had to go in and grind up the hunks. We raked and raked and raked until we opened the season in that ball park. We didn't have any grass. It was all dirt and there were no stands in those days. We worked all night to put up the footing [for the grandstand].

For the first home game, the field was nothing more than a flat piece of hard ground. There were no dugouts, no grandstands, no refreshment stands. But, as one player said, "Chanhassenites were prouder than New Yorkers are of the mammoth Yankee stadium."

The Red Birds played in the SCS League. Other teams included Norwood, Arlington, Carver, Colgne, Hamburg, Green Isle and later with Chaska and Victoria. The season ran from May to August.

Reuben Bongard opened an implement store after World War II. Top: Shot shows his sons, Craig and Bruce, ca. 1955.

Below: The whole town pitched in to finish the new field and grandstand. Joe Meuwissen rakes the infield.

The Chanhassen Red Birds Baseball Team, Region 7B Champions and State Tournament Team. Photo taken in Detroit Lakes. Front row (l-r): Howard Meuwissen and Harry Bongard, Batboys. Row 2: Stan Roeser, Rube Bongard, Ole Iverson, Bogie Raser, John Dean, Frank Schneider, George Shorba, Jr., Walt Raser. Row 3: Bob Meuwissen, Gene Kramer, ? Maze, Harry Pauly, Tom Kelm, Elroy Williams (scorekeeper), Hank Bartell, Barney Riesgraf, Roger Pauly, Dennis Van Sloun.

Right: Box score for 1949 Regional Championship Game.

1949 Regional Championship Game
Chanhassen vs Morristown
at Young America
Sept. 6, 1949

Chanhassen		AB	H	PO	A
Bongard	3b	4	1	0	3
Roeser	ss	5	3	3	2
Dean	cf	5	1	2	0
B. Raser	rf	5	2	1	0
H. Pauly	lf	4	1	0	1
Bartel	1b	5	1	7	1
Schneider	c	5	2	5	0
Meuwissen	2b	3	0	3	1
R. Pauly	p	4	0	1	1

Morristown		AB	H	PO	A
Meshelke	ss	4	2	0	2
Snyder	2b	4	1	2	1
Zitzman	cf	4	2	2	0
Meshelke	3b	4	0	2	1
Borchardt	1b-p	4	0	6	0
Wolf	lf	3	0	1	0
Ulen	rf	3	1	0	1
Rasmussen	c	2	1	7	0
Allen	c	1	0	1	0
Wagner	rf	2	0	0	0
Huber	p	1	0	1	5

Chanhassen 002 000 400-6
Morristown 000 000 001-1

Runs, Bongard 2, Roeser 2, Dean, B. Raser Snyder, Runs batted in B. Raser 4, Dean 2, Zitzman. Two base hits, H. Pauly, B. Raser, Roeser Bartel, Rasmussen. Sac. Meuwissen, hit by pitcher Huber (Meuwissen, H. Pauly) Struck Out, by R. Pauly 7 by Huber 3 by Borchardt 5. Bases on Balls, off Pauly 1, off Huber 2. Time 2:05, Umpires, Zilynski and Olsen, scorer, Williams. Winning pitcher, R. Pauly, loser, Borchardt.

Bongard chose the players, although some were obvious selections. They were mostly town boys. As Cy Kerber complained, "Farmer kids had less time to practice." Everyone was a Catholic except for Hank Bartel, a kid from Eden Prairie, Hank. The team made its debut on May 4, 1947 when they beat Hydes Lakes by a score of 9–4. In the starting lineup were Hank Bartel, shortstop; Manager Rube Bongard, second base; Fred Miller, first base; John Dean, centerfield; Bob Meuwissen, right field; Frank Schneider, catcher; and Stan Roeser, pitcher. Rube was a good showman. Ron Roeser said, "Rube had a lot of tricks. He kicked the ball into the corn field and came right out again. He'd used to swing two bats and then went up with that leaded bat and would act like he forgot. It was kind of showbizzy."

The town caught Redbird fever. Ron Roeser recalls, "All of a sudden there were real heroes in town." Cy Kerber said, "Baseball was our first love. It was next to God because you went to mass on Sunday and then you played baseball." "If you wanted to rob the town," said Tom Kelm, "you just waited until Sunday afternoon." The first year they wound up in fourth place and were eliminated after one game of the playoffs. Ron Roeser said, "Everybody was excited about it. Claude Sinnen had a great big old army truck and he used to haul all the kids. The season ran from May to August and with the playoffs it would run a little bit later." A thousand fans showed up for games, more for the playoffs. All this in a town of less than two hundred.

Father Oswald became a big fan and often sat on the bench with his Redbird cap. The nuns, Tom Kelm remembered, used to sit on their back porch and watch the game. "When the Red Birds fell behind," he said, "one of the sisters would run up to the chapel and say a prayer." Those prayers were answered in the great year of 1949.

In 1949 the Red Birds advanced to the state tournament behind the pitching of Roger Pauly, the home run power of Harry Pauly and the clutch hitting of Bogie Raser. They swept by Green Isle and Mound in the playoffs and rolled over Hollywood, Plato and Morristown to reach the state amateur tournament in Detroit Lakes. But Ulen rallied for three runs in the top of the ninth to win ten to nine. There were many good years but if youth must face one moment of regret, for Chanhassen boys it came during the 1949 playoffs. Bogie Raser lamented, "We had a good team the year we went to the state tournament. I don't know what happened there. It was a bad call."

Raser calls the play: "Reuben was playing third base and he threw a ball over there and it looked to me like it was on time. The umpire calls the guy safe. We're one run ahead at the time." Ron Roeser thought the play shook up the coach. "Rube made a couple of errors but he really fell apart after that because he kept creeping up closer to

The Schutrops owned the Feed Mill and built the elevator in 1945. Far left: Ivo Schutrop. Second left: Hank Schutrop, owner.

the line every time they hit a ball to him. He had six or seven errors that game."

Rube quit managing in 1958 and Raser took over. In a recent interview, Raser said, "I might still be playing if Florence (his wife) hadn't stopped me!" And if you ask respectfully, some old Red Birds might show you their team jacket, stored carefully in the closet.

American Legion Hall

Gene Coulter, Reuben Bongard, and several other veterans organized an American Legion post after the war. In 1954 they built a hall for their meetings. Dutch Pauly remembered.

The American Legion built a hall in 1953. This building was later converted into the Riviera. this photograph was taken on Memorial Day, 1955.

Father Oswald Gasper, right, talks with Arthur Dagman, first commander of the Legion. Roy Roeser is the boy on the far right.

We decided to build. No money. Bill Kerber was going to sell us the piece of property up there. I was finance officer and I gave him a check for $650 and said don't cash it. I got a bingo game going. Gene Coulter and I ran the bingo game and we made $1400. I told Bill Kerber, "Now you can cash the check." We all laid the floor, poured our own cement. I said anybody that's going to tear that down is going to have a problem. The first New Year's Eve Party we packed them in there.We had a band from New Ulm and they couldn't get on the stage.

This men, one person remembers, were the shakers and movers. "There was not a lot of dissension," he said. "All those people ran the town more or less. They were a pretty tight knit group."

Saint Huberts

Even the priest was a veteran. Father Oswald Gasper, a former chaplain in the Army, came to Saint Hubert's Church in 1949. He is still remembered as the priest who eliminated the outhouses. They installed flush toilets in the basement of the old school. Frank Kurvers remembered, "Father motivated the parish community to donate a total of $90 a Sunday to raise $25,000 to redecorate the old church. The new face-lift to the inside included painting all the ceilings and walls with artwork, adding gold leaf to the altars, pulpit, confessional and communion rail, carpet on the sanctuary floor, padding on the kneelers, and even a few light fixtures were added." An electronic Wulitzer organ was installed. Ron Roeser said, "He was a new breed of Franciscan."

As the baby boom hit Chanhassen, increased attendance crowded the classrooms. For a time, seventh and eighth graders were bussed to Guardian Angels in Chaska. Fr. Oswald's successor, Father Herbert Diethelm, decided that a new school was needed. He organized a building committee and appointed Gene Coulter as chairman. As usual, Coulter pushed through a new building. Dutch Pauly remem-

Saint Hubert's built a new school in 1955. The church was added in 1974.

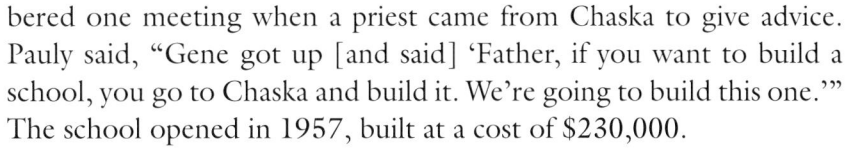

bered one meeting when a priest came from Chaska to give advice. Pauly said, "Gene got up [and said] 'Father, if you want to build a school, you go to Chaska and build it. We're going to build this one.'" The school opened in 1957, built at a cost of $230,000.

Father Herbert was followed by Father Firmin Weber. Father Firmin stayed for sixteen years. He was, as a parishioner said, "a hardworking, stubborn, reverent, irascible priest who knew what he wanted and knew where he was going." Frank and Myrna Kurvers wrote, "when he arrived the parish was $210,000 in debt to pay for the new school. When he left he had not only paid it off but had raised a considerable sum for the new church."

Business

Across the street, the State Bank of Chanhassen went through some changes as well. Elmer Kelm was appointed as Collector of Customs in Minnesota, a coveted patronage job. Since he had less time to spend at the bank, he hired Frank Schneider in 1946. Schneider had owned a hardware store in Victoria then worked for Land O'Lakes Creameries as auditor.

He bought the bank from Kelm in the early fifties and hired his son, Bernard, as Assistant Cashier. He remained at the State Bank of Chanhassen until his retirement as President and Chairman of the Board in 1972. As banker in a quiet town, Schneider was at the center of two of its most exciting events: bank robberies. In 1948 a thief stole $1,450.00 but was apprehended within an hour of the holdup. In September 1957 a bandit held up the bank and took $1,500.00. The thief hit Schneider on the head with a pistol, then dragged him into the vault. Frank found an old wrench and started banging the pipes.

Bernard (top) and Charles Schneider took over the State Bank of Chanhassen from their father in 1965.

They heard it down at Pauly's Bar and came to rescue him. They never caught the robber. Schneider sold the bank to his sons in 1965.

In 1958 A. V. Krueger and Dallas Capesius faced a tough business loss when their Shakopee restaurant burned to the ground. They approached the Chanhassen American Legion the next year and worked out a purchase for their hall. The Riviera opened in 1959 as a "private bottle" club. Since it did not have a liquor license, members were given a private locker to store their bottle. One long time employee, Joanne Meuwissen recalled, "We were only open four nights a week when the Riv opened. Then, after twelve and a half years, the son of one of the original owners bought it and opened it to the public. I've only had two bosses up there. We had the same waitresses. They all had been there 20, 25, 30 years and we were like a family." It is still operated by "Skinny" Krueger's son and daughter-in-law, Tom and Lou Krueger.

In the early 1960s, Ed Hjermstad came to town and bought out the Fairway franchise from the Dutch Pauly, opening the Colonial Center across the street. It introduced the "strip" shopping center to Chanhassen. Just north of town, Bob Scholer built the first subdivision—Sunrise Hills—in White Bill Kerber's pasture. Scholer came to Chanhassen through his marriage to Celine Kerber and bought his father-in-law's property. Since Chanhassen had a notorious water problem, he put in the first community well system for his development. In later years, the city purchased the well and added the water tower.

The Riviera took over the American Legion Hall and opened as a private bottle club in 1959.

Herb Bloomberg

Herbert Bloomberg was another World War II veteran who changed Chanhassen. Bloomberg grew up in Minneapolis. He was filled with an inner drive, even as a boy. He recalled,

> I was pretty good with door to door stuff. Dad was out of work in the early 1920s. I had some cards printed up and took some and went to the door bells and said, "I have a father who is a good carpenter and he can do anything in building." That same evening we started getting telephone calls. The second day, they told me that I couldn't do that anymore because he had too many jobs.

Herb was ten at the time.

After World War II, Bloomberg began several housing developments in Edina. As that suburb grew, though, available land became harder to find. Bloomberg recalled, "I got married and built this first

The village installed new street lights in 1963. Mayor George Buschkowsky (right) throws the switch. He is joined by Henry Dimler, President of the Chamber of Commerce (center) and Bill Curry (left), a representative of NSP.

house in Edina and managed to scrape up enough to invest a little so I could get some land. I knew we were running out."

He ended up in Chanhassen because of a farm owner's tears. He remembered,

> I came very close to buying the Holasek Farm on Bryant Lake [in Eden Prairie]. I went to the door and said, "Well I guess we decided to buy your farm." She …started to cry because she …didn't want to sell. She said, "Why don't you look at my husband's brother's place out on Lotus Lake in Chanhassen." We drove out on No. 5, just a dirt road out here. We drove right out there, we didn't even go home.
>
> I drove up No. 101 and saw the house and Herb Holasek. Apparently he wanted to get away. He wanted to sell it. He really wanted to get out of the resort business. He took me for a walk through the property. It was a mile of lakeshore and 120 acres and was for sale for $64,000. I went home that night with Carol and I said, "This is one of those deals where you don't do any bargaining. This is a good deal." I went right out and put down a couple thousand dollars and made arrangements to buy it.
>
> I came back a few weeks later and…sat down across the desk from Herb Hagen [the realtor] and said, "I suppose it wasn't the smartest to pay the first asking price for the property." And he pushed his chair back and pulled out of his desk a check for $5,000. "Well," he said, "here's somebody who thought they were going to get it for less." Apparently it had been on the market and people looked at it and didn't make up their minds.

Bloomberg built his own home there and began the Colonial Grove development. Chanhassen, he found, had a small town atmosphere. When he wanted to put in a road, he questioned his attorney, William Odell. "I told him I'd been living in Edina and they had some rules. He said, 'Well, you own the land, don't you?'"

Carol Bloomberg described her husband as "very energetic and enthusiastic. He's very much a free thinker and doer. You can't regulate anything. He's very very creative." Where did the ideas come from? Bloomberg said, "I can't tell you how an artist can paint a picture...I did the same thing with building architecture...build it, rebuild it, or remodel it. Just naturally. You don't work at it." In many ways, the village of Chanhassen became his greatest project.

Frontier Village

Once settled, the Bloombergs began to shake up old Chanhassen. Carol Bloomberg reacted to the town, saying, "There was very little out here when we first moved. There was no public school in Chanhassen and there was no other church other than the Catholic Church."

It was hard to find supplies for their construction business so they bought land in town and opened Frontier Lumber in 1959. Carol Bloomberg said, "We really bought for our own purposes of building. We were able to acquire more property and we built the lumber yard and hardware store and the furniture store." Carol Bloomberg said, "People used to come get lumber and write a note and say, 'I took two

Herb and Carol Bloomberg

Downtown Chanhassen, ca. 1960.

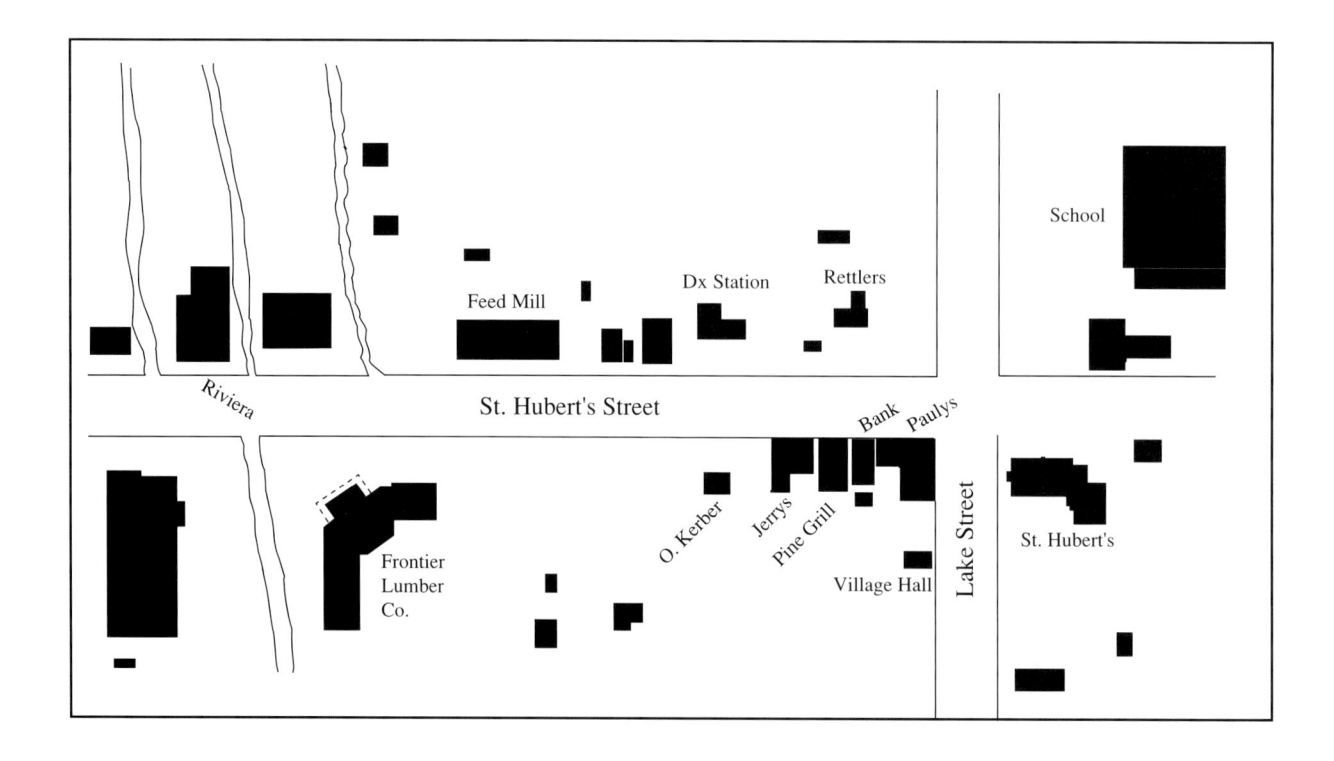

Herbert and Carol Bloomberg moved to Chanhassen in 1956. When his construction business demanded supplies, Bloomberg built the Frontier Lumber Company which opened in 1959. Top: Frontier Lumber. The Riviera is on the left.

boards today' and sign their name. People all worked on the honor system."

Herb had big ideas for the little town. "Chanhassen," he told a *Minneapolis Star* reporter, "is probably going to be another Southdale." Herb and Carol Bloomberg traveled to Arizona one year and came away with a love for the western architecture in Scottsdale. He designed his lumber yard in a rustic motif and encouraged other store owners to join with him. It was accepted with almost shocking ease. As Adolph Tessness remembered, "Anything Herb wanted the City would do. The main street and his style of building. Everything had to look like his type of building." Suddenly the old Germans sported cowboy hats and the village was promoted as "The Western–most Town in Minnesota."

Bloomberg's energy closed the deal as did his willingness to invest in Chanhassen. In 1961 the Bloombergs opened a furniture store and a hardware store. A local committee began Frontier Days, using the Wild West theme, an annual celebration that featured a parade, mock hangings, and a variety of special events. Tessness remembered, "The local people like Ed Hjermstad, Jim Thompson, Bernie Schneider, and Harry Pauly were probably the prime movers because it was commercially oriented. The residents disliked the noise, traffic. We had a carnival. We were going to hang Ed Hjermstad (in a mock lynching) but we couldn't lift him because he was too heavy." It became the major community event for a decade.

168 Chanhassen: A Centennial History

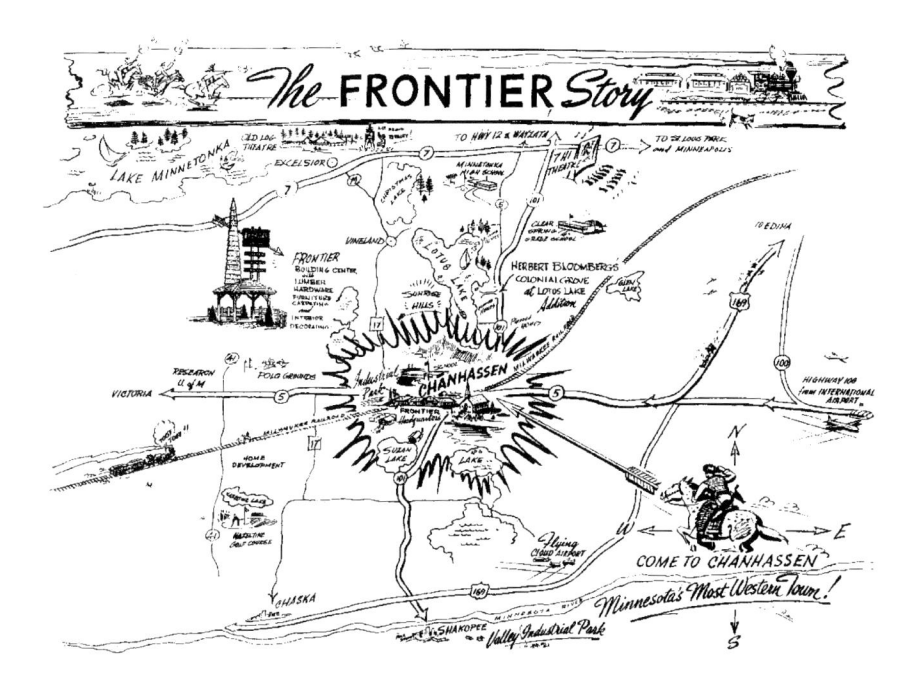

Opposite Page
Top: Hubert Humphrey was the guest of honor at the 1970 Frontier Days parade. He was joined by Loretta Kelm and Emil Pauly.

Lower Left: Lorraine Hanson, Lorraine Roeser and Vernice Jorrisen dressed up for Frontier Days.

Lower Right: Donnie Rettler watches the parade. He is standing in front of Bongards Implement.

Mayor Coulter

If Herb Bloomberg brought a visionary's drive to the town, it found its match in the energy of Gene Coulter. When George Buschkowsky finally stepped down as mayor in 1963, Coulter became a consensus choice to lead the city government. It came at a time when the pace of activity quickened. His wife said, "It was a hectic time. There was no city clerk and we got the complaints at our house. The kids dreaded suppertime because there were so many complaints.He would come home and eat and be off to a meeting."

His wife remembered, "He liked to see things develop and he saw that the town was at a standstill. He had so much ambition that you could not hold him down."

One former council member said, "He was driven. He never stood still. He could never stand things being settled. He always had to do more. The day of the lazy main street…was gone. We didn't even have a building code in town. Gene conceived the problems that would develop if we kept doing this. So that is why he adopted codes and ordinances and just really got rolling. The timing was perfect. People liked him. He was kind-hearted."

1965 Tornado

Where were you on the evening of May 6, 1965? Herb Bloomberg remembers standing at the window when it looked as if the water from Lotus Lake had taken to the air. He called Adolph Tessness. Tessness had worse luck. His house was gone.

At Jerry's Bar, Joe Hedtke, the bartender, was coming in for the evening shift when he spotted the funnel cloud. He ran in the door,

The 1965 tornado ripped through town near the dinner hour. Frontier Lumber suffered major damage. Schlenk's Gas Station had the rear wall blown away. Fortunately, there were no fatalities.

shouting, "Everybody downstairs! There's a tornado coming." Tom O'Laughlin, the daytime bartender, said, "When I saw Joe running downstairs, I figured he was serious and dashed after him." The customers grabbed their beers and ran to the basement. It missed the bar but all the lights went out. Across the street the tornado ripped through Jerry Schlenk's gas station, ripping out the rear wall. Six homes were destroyed and ten more were severly damaged. Much of the Frontier Center was destroyed with lumber strewn like Pick-Up-Sticks.

Gwen Pearson remembered,

> I cooked a chicken dinner and was getting ready to put it on the table when it started hailing outside big as golf balls. After it stopped the children wanted to go out and collect them. While we were out in the yard, I saw these big black clouds in the south, then saw the funnel cloud.
>
> I hurried the children into the southwest corner of the basement then waited. Then we heard it. It was a very loud roar and we could hear glass flying upstairs. The basement windows blew out above us. Then it was quiet again. We went upstairs and all we saw was blue sky. The piano is almost ready to fall out of the house and there's a lawn chair way up in a tree. It was real freakish. The goldfish are still swimming around in the bowl back there in the southwest corner bedroom–the only room in the house that wasn't damaged.

Rita Rojina was downstairs ironing. "You could see it over the trees. It circled and was hitting Lotus Lake and then jumping over to Christmas Lake. I spent the next three hours in the basement under a table." A block away, Ron Roeser heard his children shouting.

> The kids were outside and they said something. I could hear this in the distance and I was looking right out this window. There were sparks flying and there was dirt flying and I was watching the Mileage Station blow away. We ran outside and we could hear this roaring and see this huge black cloud moving towards Lotus Lake. It took Adolph's house out completely. The National Guard came out and blocked off streets.

It hit the Klingelhutz farm south of town. Roeser recalled, "They looked out the window and it was pitch black and he got all of the kids in the basement and they heard this tremendous crash and part of the barn flew into the house and kicked the cupboards just off the wall. They had a really close call."

Miraculously, no one was seriously injured.

Minnesota Landscape Arboretum

In early 1955 the Minnesota Horticultural Society appointed a committee to study the need for an arboretum and for increased research in the field of hardy wood ornamentals. On March 3, 1955, the committee recommended action triggering the authorization of a Landscape Arboretum. A major fundraising campaign followed. Within a year, the society purchased an option on a tract of 160 acres near the Fruit Breeding Farm. After a successful fundraising campaign, the property was given to the University of Minnesota.

Above: The Arboretum raised funds through membership drives. This photograph was taken in 1963.

Right: The magnificent building was designed by architect Edward Lundy.

The first of two new fire trucks was put into service in March 1971. Miss Flame, Janet Kerber, goes for a ride.

The arboretum was the child of Dr. Leon C. Snyder. Snyder was born in Michigan and joined the University of Minnesota in 1945 as extension horticulturalist. In the fifties, Snyder was living in Chanhassen, directing the Department of Horticultural Science and superintendent of the University Fruit Breeding Farm. He headed the department from 1953 to 1970. In 1958 he was named Director of the Minnesota Landscape Arboretum. In 1970 he devoted full time to the Arboretum. Snyder was a great popularizer of plants, writing a weekly gardening column in the *Minneapolis Tribune* and producing programs for WCCO.

It seemed to be a risk in committing the future of the Arboretum to Chanhassen but Snyder knew many local families. Jean Sinnen, who worked at the Experimental Farm for a year, said, "Doctor Snyder had a vision that a lot of people just never had. Forty years ago, they thought, well, what's so big about having a farm with some plants on it? We have lots of farms around here with plants on it." In some ways, the Arboretum was the final fruition of the work of Henry Lyman in the previous century.

A fire destroyed Harold Kerber's barn on August 25, 1964. It was located where McDonald's and the Chanhassen Estates neighborhood are today. The event inspired Mayor Coulter to organize a local fire department.

Fire Department

On August 25, 1964 Harold Kerber's barn burned down. Since it was the end of summer, the barn was filled with almost ten thousand bales of dry alfalfa and hay. The blaze was spectacular. It was clear that Chanhassen needed a fire department.

The volunteer fire department held their first meeting in May, 1966. Earl McAllister remembered, "We received a notice from the Excelsior Fire Department…that they would be unable to serve us because…if they had a call at the same time that we had a fire here that they would have to respond to their call and ours would be left until later."

Mayor Coulter suggested a local fire department to several men in the community and a meeting was held in May 1966 at the Legion Hall. Thirty men signed up. At the first meeting on May 16, they elected officers, including Fire Chief Jim Thompson, Assistant Chief Bill Robertson, Earl McAllister, Fire Marshal, and Tom Klingelhutz, Drillmaster.

The new department purchased a 1950 Dodge tanker from Golden Valley for $2,600. Golden Valley "threw in a few helmets and a few boots," McAllister remembered. "Tom Klingelhutz sold the unit an old mail truck for a dollar. The truck was converted into a rescue vehicle. The volunteers rented an old garage just off of Main Street. That's where we held our first training meetings."

In the middle of the 1960s, Chanhassen was still a small town but undergoing rapid changes in many unseen ways. It was still a rural village. Jim Klobuchar could write in the *Minneapolis Star* that, "Nobody overwhelms Chanhassen very quickly. It has pursued its addiction to the past with ardor, knocking the hell out of much of the twentieth century's inroads here in the process."

The inroads included the rush of urban development, requiring better roads, schools and sewers. In 1967 Chanhassen approved the construction of a new village hall. Kay Klingelhutz recalled the hectic spring of 1965.

> I started as Clerk–Treasurer. The City never had a budget. Gene said we are going to do a budget so Gene, Russ Larson, and I would meet at our kitchen table and do all our business. They decided to have a fire deparment so we had the first fire department meeting in our basement—Earl, Jim, Howie Meuwissen. The first part of April, Chaska floods out so we have to send firemen to Chaska. The fifth of May the tornado hit. We were trying to get a grant to get the sewer plant replaced and then in June they start putting in city water and it rains and rains and the street is all mud.

Events in the township, already underway, would soon lead to an even greater change.

Chapter Ten
One Chanhassen

JEAN SINNEN REMEMBERED THE CONFUSION. "We lived in Chanhassen Township," she wrote, "got mail at the Chanhassen Post Office and had a Shakopee telephone exchange. Chaska had the public school system, and we went to the Public Library at Glen Lake." In the 1960s, the residents of Chanhassen had to chose and define their future. Did they wish to split up and attach themselves to surrounding communities? Did they want to maintain their own identity? The question was the same one that had faced the Northampton Colonists. They wanted to see New England transferred to Minnesota. It was the question faced by the early German and Dutch Catholic settlers. They chose to build a community centered around their church, apart from the surrounding culture. What kind of a community do we want?

The debate started in 1961. When the population of a township passes 2,000, the Minnesota Municipal Commission (MMC) is required to hold hearings to determine its legal future, Chanhassen Township was the largest piece of unincorporated land in Carver County and became a target for the competing interests of local governments.

Chaska made the first move, petitioning to annex 3,800 acres of Chanhassen Township, including the new Hazeltine Golf Course and the proposed "New Town" developed by McKnight Corporation. After a year of study and debate, the MMC approved the annexation. In one legal manuever, Chanhassen lost its southwest corner. The township board was outraged and fought the ruling all the way to the Minnesota Supreme Court where they lost. Victoria began considerations to annex the northwest corner.

Richard Lyman, the grandson of Henry and the son of Arthur, was chairman of the township board at the time. Adolph Tessness recalls Lyman's attitude. "Chanhassen owes a great debt to Dick Lyman. He was one of the strongest advocates. He did not want to see Chanhassen dissected and end up nothing. When Dick Lyman saw Jonathan take a big slice. His feeling was that Excelsior would come down and take a pinch off another end and the core of old Chanhassen would grow slightly but never grow into something viable." To stem the flow, the township board filed a petition to incorporate as the village of Minnewashta on September 30, 1965.

Behind the scenes, Lyman and Al Klingelhutz, a newly-elected supervisor, negotiated with Gene Coulter to merge with the village of Chanhassen. Klingelhutz recalls,

> I met with Gene Coulter and said, 'I wonder if there isn't a possibility that we could merge the township and village.' There was a lot of resentment among the agricultural people because the city's taxes were considerably higher. We got a promise to establish a rural urban taxing district so that the land of the farms would be taxed at virtually the same rate.

Bloomberg commissioned this drawing of his vision of a revitalized downtown Chanhassen in 1965. It is still relatively modest and does not include the Dinner Theatre.

In the end, it was the agreement between Gene Coulter, the member of the old Pauly family that first donated land for Saint Hubert's Church, and Dick Lyman, grandson of a member of the Northampton Colony, that sealed the deal.

Reading their signals, the MMC issued an order in December 1967 that the township and village would merge if there were no objections within the community. The first municipal elections were scheduled for early April. As the deadline approached, a local ad hoc group filed a petition, signed by six hundred residents, requesting a referendum. A flurry of legal manuevers followed as signatures were challenged by the township lawyers. A vote was scheduled for May 2, 1967.

Opposition developed among two groups. There was some concern among the older residents of the village that they would be swallowed up and lose control. Adolph Tessness remembered, "At Pauly's there was a lot of outspoken [opposition]." He credits Wally Hanson, Gene Coulter and Ron Roeser with easing the concerns of the village residents.

Some of the residents of the Lake Minnewashta community opposed the merger as well. "They had a feeling that they were part of Excelsior," said Tessness. "And that Chanhassen was not a very enlightened community. There wasn't much there but Pauly's." Ada Anding recalled, "I was mad. We had all our dealings with Excelsior. It would have been better if it had been left that way." Among her concerns, the Excelsior Fire Department would not respond promptly to fire alarms in a different city and Chanhassen's department was too far away.

On May 2nd, the merger was approved by a two to one vote. Chanhassen Township was dissolved. There were some additional issues for residents closer to Chaska and Victoria. Henry Wrase remembered,

Richard and Mary Lyman. Richard was the Chairman of the Township Board of Supervisors at the time of the merger with the village.

> There were about four of us that had an opportunity to vote whether we wanted to stay with Chanhassen Township or go to the City of Chaska. That became a problem when McKnight

Chanhassen built its first public school in 1967. This photograph shows the start of construction.

came and bought all of this property and started McKnight Development [Jonathan]. So we voted to stay in Chanhassen. My neighbor south of me voted to go to Chaska. I don't know if there were a lot of ill feelings. It was just a fact of life that both cities wanted to set a dividing line to be fair to each one of them.

The township permanently lost sections to Chaska and Victoria. There was now one Chanhassen. The jump from a sprawling township and a sleepy little village into a merged municipality put Chanhassen into the modern village class. The new city encompassed approximately twenty-four square miles of land and a population of 4112 people, the largest town in Carver County. Elections were held within weeks. Gene Coulter, unopposed, was elected mayor. Al Klingelhutz, Hibbert Hill, James Bennyhoff, and Adolph Tessness were elected trustees. Bennyhoff, a dentist, lived in the Minnewashta area and helped ease that section's concerns. Dick Lyman lost in his bid for a trustee seat.

Coulter began the task of creating a new government. Adolph Tessness recalled, "Chanhassen was almost in Abe Lincoln's days in all reality." Planning, at least in the township days, was non-existent.

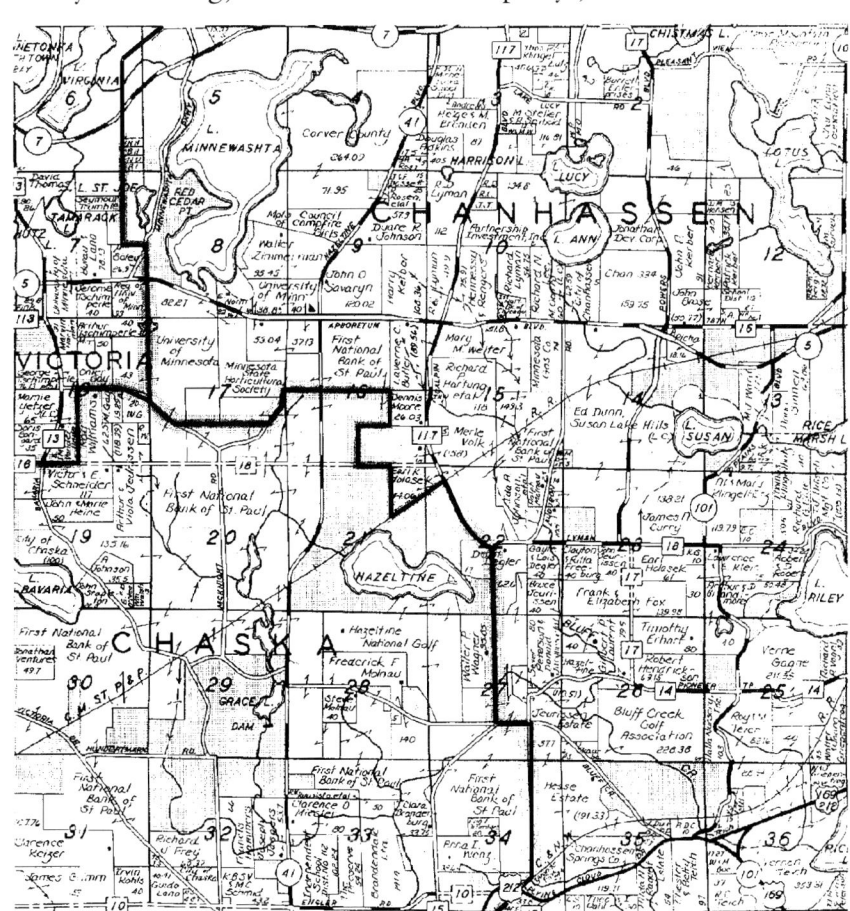

The merger and annexation votes divided the township between Victora, Chaska, and the new city of Chanhassen.

Al Klingelhutz remembered,

> I saw footings for houses going in down on Pioneer Trail which I knew flooded every spring. So I went to a township board meeting. I said, "What are you guys doing letting houses be built in swamps that flood?" They gave building permits without going out and looking at the sites and I was pretty upset about it.

Coulter hired Tessness as a full-time administrator. He appointed a planning commission. The city agreed to join the Southwest Sanitary Sewer District. Tessness recalled those days, "When I was hired, we didn't have a building inspector, plumbing inspector, or a dog catcher. Jerry Schlenk was made the building inspector. Jerry Boucher was hired and kind of worked his way away from the utility department."

In 1969, the village purchased a sixty-three acre park on Lake Ann. Klingelhutz pushed through the purchase option. He said, "One of my favorite accomplishments was Lake Ann Park. The land was owned by the Welters. I told the children that if they ever wanted to sell, I wished to talk. I thought it was the most beautiful spot in Chanhassen for a park. We negotiated with them and acquired the farm through a referendum."

As a result of the merger vote, Chanhassen gained a major industry. The M.A. Gedney Company petitioned for inclusion in the new city one week after the May 2nd vote. Although the company had long been associated with Chaska, the company opted for the lower tax rate of their northern neighbor. Mattias Gedney began the compnay in 1881 in Minneapolis. Over the years, they expanded the original building and built a sauerkraut and pickle plant in Chaska. In 1958 the company moved its headquarters and pickle operations to Chaska. The vinegar plant moved to Chanhassen in 1981.

Chanhassen was one of the first communities to join the Southwest Sanitary Sewer District (SSSD). The *Chaska Weekly Herald*, Oct 23, 1969, warned, "The advent of this sewer facility will open a Pandora's Box. It is conceivable that the village could double in size within five years." It was a divisive issue within the community. Sewer and water lines control where development takes place and have important economic impacts on land values and taxes. Tessness said,

> I think that by not extending sewer and water down into the southern part of Hwy 5 kept that a more rural nature for as long as possible. In the northern areas where there was agricultural land, it was pretty much determined that development was going to continue. I didn't feel that we had any strong objection from some of the larger agricultural land owners.

Al Klingelhutz, member of an old Chanhassen family, served on the Township Board of Supervisors and the new Chanhassen City Council. He was elected mayor in 1972.

Dinner Theater

Herb and Carol Bloomberg were ready to test a new idea on Chanhassen. Several years before, Herb had built the Old Log Theater in Excelsior. He liked the dinner theater concept and the seeds for the Chanhassen Dinner Theatres were planted. Don Stoltz, who managed the Old Log, joined with Bloomberg in the planning stages and worked to obtain a local liquor license—a key piece of the economic plan. There was a sharp debate in Chanhassen. One community leader said,

> The liquor license became a pretty hot topic because Herb Bloomberg at many times would start things and go off on tangents. He almost didn't get his liquor license. The community of old Chanhassen only accepted Herb Bloomberg at that stage of the game because he was there, but they didn't accept him as a friend of any kind or as a part of the community. He just happened to own a piece of land but they didn't feel he was a part of the community.

The Riviera and the Legion both wanted the one available liquor license and could show immediate results. The Bloombergs' plan would not see fruition for several years. But it was a big idea and that sold the city council. The theatre faced one more crisis before it opened. Don Stoltz had the opportunity to buy the Old Log Theatre and took it. Without his partnership, the Bloombergs had to decide whether to push forward. Carol Bloomberg remembered, "We were left with this structure and having to make the decision of whether to move or not and we did. We just went ahead."

In 1968, Bloomberg opened the Chanhassen Dinner Theatre across the street from the feedmill. At least Ole Kerber's cows were no longer roaming the streets. The first production was the musical, "How to Succeed in Business Without Really Trying." It was a huge gamble. Many of the local residents never thought it would work. "He had to convince people that driving to the theater wasn't like driving to Yankton, S.D.," said Bill McRostie, vice president of Bloomberg Cos. "Herb was interested in theater and music; he thought that it would be a good business but a lot of people didn't believe it."

Bloomberg remembered the early days. He said, "Initially the theater was tough sledding. We were a thinly financed business and we ran into some horrendous losses." To stay afloat he sold out 200 acres of real estate. Even in later years, Bloomberg said, "I treat it like the stock market."

Carol Bloomberg tried to place the theatre in perspective in a 1991 interview. She said, "The theater wasn't the major part of our lives. It really only played a small part. I think we've done a lot for the

180   Chanhassen: A Centennial History

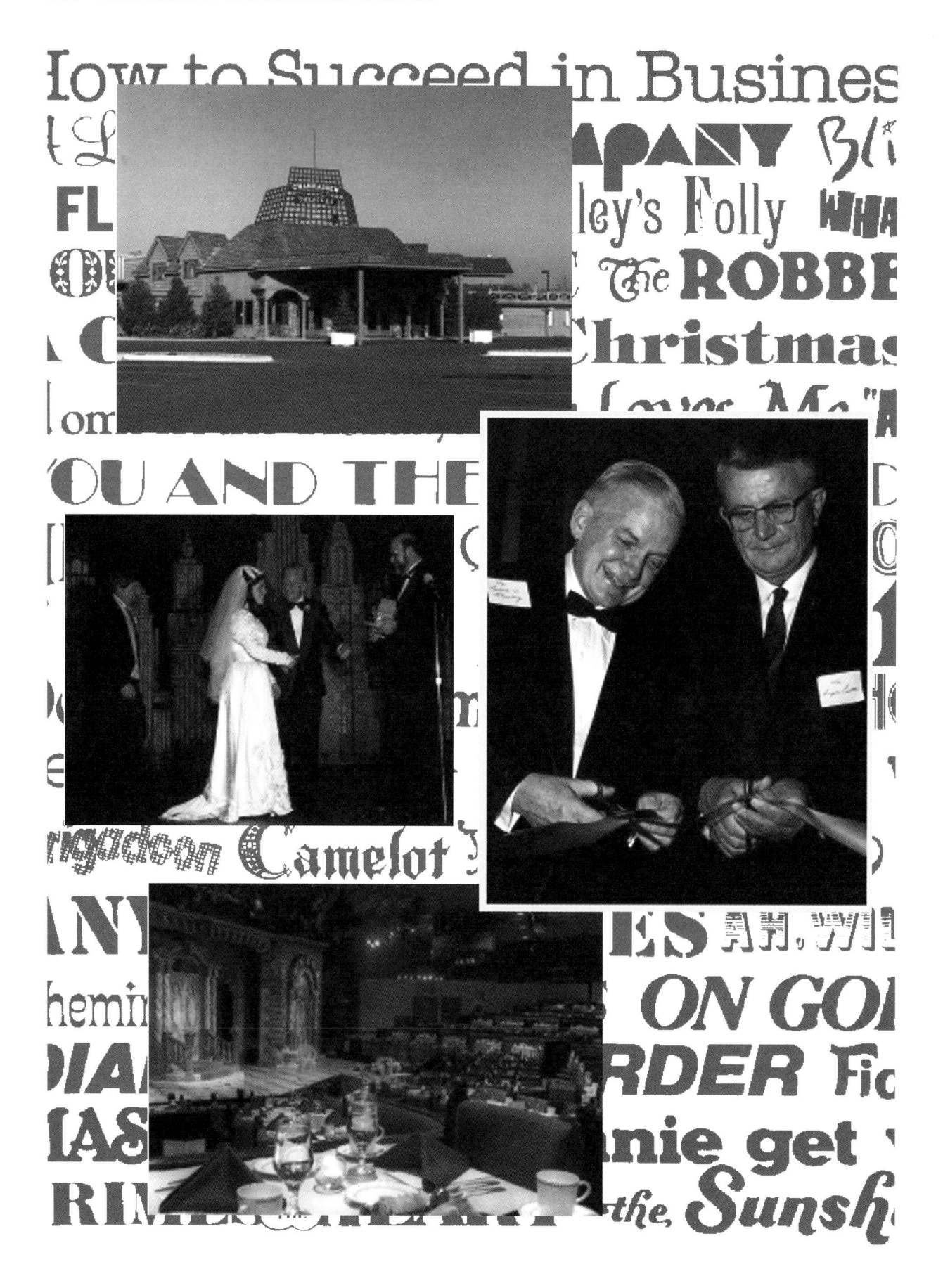

The Chanhassen Civic Theater carried on a thespian tradition in the community., dating back to the St. Hubert's Dramatic Club. This photograph shows a 1972 production of "Annie Get Your Gun" with Ron Roeser. It was staged at Saint Hubert's School.

Opposite page:
Top and Lower:
Chanhassen Dinner Theatre

Right, center: Herbert Bloomberg and Mayor Gene Coulter cut the ribbon to open the new Chanhassen Dinner Theater on October 14, 1968.

Left, center: At the fifteenth anniversary celebration of the Chanhassen Dinner Theatre, Herb Bloomberg and Gary Gisselman congratulate David Anders and Susan Goeppinger, the cast of "I Do! I Do!" The production continued for a record twenty-two and a half years.

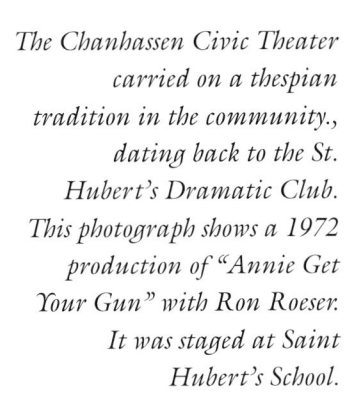

community and actually that's always been our goal. Herb and I have never really done anything for ourselves. It gave us a good cash flow...but it never brought us any great number of dollars. It certainly helped other dinner theaters perhaps gain some respect because dinner theater in general is kind of sneered on."

The concept worked. The history of the dinner theatre requires its own book, detailing the productions, the staff, the business strategies, and more. Bloomberg built additional theatres and experimented with other concepts such as the Bronco Bar. But for the first time, Chanhassen had name recognition beyond its borders. In previous years, when local residents talked about the downtown, they typically answered, "There's not much there. A grocery store. Two bars." Now when people say that they are from Chanhassen, people will respond, "Oh, the dinner theatre!"

Village to City: The Political Transition

The political transition from township and village to city continued for several years. Al Klingelhutz was elected mayor in 1972. The position of mayor required a tremendous commitment of time and the work load kept increasing. Klingelhutz recalled,

> Being a farmer and being on the city council wasn't so easy. I remember one time I had about a twenty acre corn field all ready to plant. In fact, I started planting on it and it got to be about 7:30. I had to quit for a city council meeting. That night it rained about four inches and I didn't get back to the field for about three weeks. The corn I planted turned out beautifully. The rest was poorer.

Don Ashworth was hired as city administrator in early 1976. Ashworth was a native of South Dakota and earned a Master of Public Administration degree from the University of Kansas. Ashworth had worked with many of the issues confronting a fringe suburb while assistant city manager and finance director in Maplewood. With Ashworth on the staff, Klingelhutz and the council decided to face the issue of professional management.

The issue was placed on the ballot in the fall of 1976 as Plan B "providing for the council-manager form of government be adopted for the government of the city." The plan provided for a mayor and four council members that would decide policy questions and hire a city manager. The administrator, in turn, handled implementation of the approved policies including the hiring of personnel. Although it was not a sharply devisive issue, since most suburbs were shifting to the city manager form of government, there was some dissension based on a desire to keep decision in the hands of "the people" through elected officials. In November Plan B won by a vote of 1483 to 1092.

As one long time resident said, "We needed a manager the way the town was growing. We needed professional inspectors that were available not just after 4:30 when the plumbing inspector got off work. Al turned the city into professional people."

Klingelhutz did not run for re-election that fall. Walter Hobbs, a sales representative for Owens-Illinois, was elected mayor over Frank Kurvers by a vote of 1450 to 1156. It was an important transition. Klingelhutz was from one of the old Chanhassen families and attended Saint Hubert's School as a boy. Hobbs and his successors represented the vast majority of city residents who had moved to the new housing developments of suburban Chanhassen.

The city acted to build new facilities. The *Carver County Herald* said in an editorial, "No question about it. Chanhassen will grow and with it, the need for more city services, offices and storage space. City records are kept now stored in hallways, damp closets, and at the unsecured Lake Ann barn." In March 1978, a referendum to finance a $795,000 city hall-public works complex was defeated. The plan was modified and submitted to the voters again in 1979. This referendum provided for a public works building, a city hall-library complex, and a satellite fire station in the northwest portion of the city. The referendum was approved by a vote of 651 to 518 on November 7, 1979.

Top: The State Bank of Chanhassen moved into a new building in 1971.

Bottom: Instant Web opened in Chanhassen on March 17, 1969. Originally located downtown, it was the first major industry to locate in the new industrial park that was created after approval of the downtown revitalization in 1980.

Three mayors. Left to right: Walter Hobbs, Tom Hamilton, Al Klingelhutz

Country to Suburb: The Economic Transition

By the mid-1970s, the first major wave of development had hit Chanhassen. It became clear that some master plan was required if the city wanted to maintain any control over its future. Herb Bloomberg had an interest, too. He wanted to see the area around his dinner theatre and Frontier Center become a strong economic magnet.

Bloomberg was appointed to head the city's Housing and Redevelopment Authority in 1976. The resulting recommendation was typical Bloomberg—no small ideas. The plan recommended that the city raze most of the downtown, replacing it with a 120 room hotel, dozens of shops, a cinema, bowling alley, gymnasium, offices, supermarket, and a town square. A ring road would be constructed around the entire central business district. Its report adopted four principal economic goals for the city:

1) Develop a business park that would attract industry;
2) Provide funding for new and aged public improvements which might otherwise retard development and/or place an additional tax burden on the community;
3) Encourage inappropriate land use within the downtown area to relocate to other areas;
4) Redevelop the downtown area to create a more viable downtown, building upon the Dinner Theatres.

Those recommendations became the defining economic document for Chanhassen. Within a few years, the first three were fully implemented. The fourth, creating a viable downtown, went through some alterations and delays but resulted in the defined shopping and business district which emerged in the past five years. The key economic engine was tax increment financing.

The report set off a public dialogue about the future of Chanhassen that lasted for four years. In a two year stretch, the city placed a moratorium on any downtown development. Some residents worried that development would ruin the local quality of life. As one woman wrote in a letter to the editor:

> When our families chose Chanhassen as our home we did so because it offered a small community and a rural quality of life. We made this choice knowing we would have to make some concessions like commuting to jobs and shopping, paying higher taxes, but this was a decision we chose to make. Must we become a Bloomington, Apple Valley or Maple Grove with the problems that accompany high density living?

The existing business people worried that they would be tossed aside in the redevelopment scheme and not receive adequate relocation costs. Some thought the plan was too grand. One voter complained, "Bloomberg's got too much pull as far as I'm concerned with City Hall."

One argument favoring the plan was that controlled growth of the downtown would provide needed services. The *Chaska Herald* said, "The need for the project is as obvious as the city's downtown, which, while providing the basics of groceries, pharmacy, beer, gas and hardware, provides little else. That means the residents of this outer ring suburb do their shopping away from home…further defining Chanhassen as a bedroom community rather than a town with its own identity."

Other supporters said that development was inevitable. If you can't stop it, make it work for you. A Chamber of Commerce press release stated,

> This attractive center offers a contrast to the typical strip development usually associated with suburban sprawl. The Chanhassen plan is designed to offer a coordinated and integrated business community that provides for the shopping and entertainment needs of the surrounding trade area. We have watched the development of the first ring of Twin Cities suburbs and their retail centers. We have seen the many different free-standing stores that have created a hodge-podge of signs, set-backs and blacktop.

On December 8th, 1980 the City Council approved the first steps of the downtown redevelopment plan. Although its next stages move beyond the parameters of this history, the concept of a distinctive

Don Ashworth took the new position of city manager in 1976.

central downtown retail and commercial center came to fruition in the early 1990s.

Don Ashworth said recently, "You look around Minnesota—the small towns are dying. Even the suburbs haven't been successful in trying to create a downtown. Smaller communities have to go with their strengths—the basic services, banking, food, post offices. You keep them downtown and you'll have downtown...You have to keep the ingredients in place for Small Town USA to be successful."

A city referendum approved three new buildings in 1979.

Top: A new city hall and library.

Middle left, Minnewashta Fire Station

Lower right: Public Works Building

The Future and the Past

Small towns are formed around landmarks—literally, buildings and places that mark the land and link the people with their past. Chanhassen landmarks suffered in the growth following the merger. Mudcura sat abandoned after the Assumption Seminary closed. Without heat in the buildings, pipes broke and the whole structure deteriorated. The feed mill lost its economic place as farms closed and in 1974, the elevator was torn down.

A central principles of the downtown redevelopment plan was the dismantling of the existing downtown. The Pony Express [Joe's] was torn down in 1995. Pauly's is scheduled for demolition. On the other hand the old Village Hall is maintained by the city and the old Milwaukee Road depot is scheduled to return downtown within a year. The Fruit Breeding Farm was recently surveyed for potential nomination as a historic district.

The effects of population growth brought new parishioners to Saint Hubert's Church. In the 1970s, Father Armand Lubanski pushed through the construction of a new church which held its first mass in September 1976. The old brick school was torn down in 1974. The future of the original church was uncertain. There was talk that the old church might be moved down to Murphy's Landing. With the building gone, some argued, the church could expand the cemetery. As one person said, "There are only about five percent of the people of Chanhassen who really have some sentimental attachment to the building." Some wanted to turn it into a community center or a branch library.

In the end the church built by John Geiser stayed on the land that the Paulys donated. As one member said, "People can see the steeple from miles away and when people enter the town they have a sense of home." Herbert and Carol Bloomberg's daughter, Britta, stepped forward to help preserve the church, completing an application to place the church on the National Register of Historic Places. It was officially designated by the Department of the Interior in 1980. That same year the city agreed to lease the building for $1 a year and it is now used by the Colonial Church at Heritage Square.

The historic core of the old village of Chanhassen includes St. Hubert's Church, the Village Hall, Klingelhutz Realty, and Pauly's. The church is listed on the National Register of Historic Places.

Since its inception, the people of Chanhassen have tried to answer the question: what kind of a community do we want? As the city celebrates the centennial of the incorporation of the village, it faces a slightly different question: how does our community—its people and its past—make us who we are? The stories of Henry Martyn Nichols and Veronica Kessler, of Arthur Lyman and Dennis Kerber, of Elmer Kelm and Albert Pauly are chapters of the same book that we continue to write today.

Opposite page: Two landmarks fell in 1974. With the changes in the local economy, the feed mill went out of business. At Saint Hubert's, the old school building went down, an event that many local residents watched and photographed.

Index

A

Aldritt 29
Aldritt, Edwin 46
Aldritt, Jemima 28
Aldritt, John 79
Alfalfadale 85, 89
Amrhein, "Mutch" 151
Arboretum 171
Ashworth, Don 182, 185
Aspden, Henry 27
Aspden, Herbert 102, 109
Aspden, John 27
Aspden, Mary 27

B

Bartel, Hank 160
Bartel, Peter 58, 60
Bender, Christian 86
Bennett, Isaac 30
Bennett, Ruth 30, 45
Bennyhoff, James 177
Bleichner, Matt 61
Bloomberg, Carol 166, 179
Bloomberg, Herbert 164, 179, 183
Bongard, Mercil 139
Bongard, Reuben 156, 157, 161
Bost, Sophie 44
Bost, Theodore
    31, 32, 34, 35, 40, 43, 45, 54, 59
Bradley, George 64
Bull, Daniel 110
Buschkowsky, George 83, 122, 169
Buschkowsky, Viola 114, 125

C

Capesius 164
Carver Beach Association 101
Cathcart, James 24
Chanhassen Dinner Theatre 179
Cheeseman, Rufus 30
Chicken Dinner 150
Christmas 153
Christmas Lake 102
Chulik, Arnold 101, 112
Civil War 45
Cleaveland 25, 26, 34, 40
Cleaveland, Arba 21, 24, 40
Cleaveland, Clarissa 33, 40
Cordell, Catherine 60
Cordell, Simon 60
Corpus Christi Day 148
Coulter, Clarice Pauly
    120, 125, 139, 146, 154
Coulter, Gene 156, 161, 169, 175, 177

D

D–X 136
Dagman, Arthur 162
Dakota War 43
Depression 107
Diethelm, Fr. Herbert 162
Dimler, Charles 71
Dimler, Henry 43, 119, 138, 146
Drasen, Frank 69, 71
drought 108
DX 122

E

Eldridge, Hiram 40
Ess, Michael 16, 17

F

Feyereisen, Peter 69
Fire Department 172
Fischer, Henry 96
Fletcher, Margaret 93
Frontier Days 167, 169
Frontier Lumber 166
Fruit Breeding Farm 90
Fuller, William 29

G

Galpin, George 24
Gasper, Fr. Oswald 162
Geiser, Charlotte 76
Geiser, Clarence 115, 129
Geiser, Fred 65, 69, 97
Geiser, John 56, 60, 71
Geiser, John C. 65
Geiser, John L. 60
Geiser, Samuel 56, 57, 58
Graftland, Rudolph 139
Griepentrog, Walter 129
Griffin, Lemuel 24

H

Hamilton, Tom 183
Hansen, Walter 139
Hanson, Lorraine 169
Haralson, Charles 91
Harrison, Edward 28
Harrison, James 79
Harvest Festival 150
Hazeltine Golf Course 174
Hazeltine, Susan 34
Henry, Dr. Fischer 97
Heutmaker, Val and Lou 156
High Path Farms 110
Hill, Hibbert 177
Hjermstad, Ed 164
Hobbs, Priscilla 108
Hobbs, Walter 182, 183
Housing and Redevelopment Authority 183
Hubertus, Saint 69
Hullsiek, Bill 139

I

Instant Web 182
Iverson, Ole 158

J

Jacques, Mary 76
Janssen, Father 62
Jeurissen, Jacob 130
Joe's 116, 121
Jorissen, Red 116, 120, 129, 131, 134
Jorisson, William 119
Jorrisen, Vernice 169
Judd, Burritt 30, 37
Judd, Clara 50, 51
Judd, William 30

K

Kelm, Douglas 123, 139, 141, 147, 150
Kelm, Elmer 133, 135, 151, 158
Kelm, Gottfried 61
Kelm, Henry 63, 133
Kelm, Rose 71
Kelm, Tom 131, 147, 158, 160
Kerber, Alois 81
Kerber, Bill 162
Kerber, Cy 101, 104, 110, 160
Kerber, Dan 79, 113
Kerber, Frank 112
Kerber, Franz 61
Kerber, Gladys
    105, 106, 107, 109, 127, 154
Kerber, Guido 139
Kerber, Harold
    104, 105, 108, 110, 133, 142, 157, 172
Kerber, Joe 120
Kerber, Julianne
    106, 107, 114, 127, 153
Kerber, Leander 104, 111
Kerber, Mause (Mouse) 137
Kerber, Mrs. Ambrose 76
Kerber, Ole 137
Kerber, Pauline 151
Kerber, Peter 112
Kerber, Peter, Mrs. 76
Kerber, Tony 105, 114, 121, 146
Kerber, William 121
Kessler 16
Kessler, Joseph 37
Kessler, Veronica 14, 17
Klein, Bernadette 9
Klein, Larry 102, 138
Klein, Willis 150
Klingelhutz, Al
    111, 171, 175, 177, 178, 181, 183
Klingelhutz, Kay 173
Klingelhutz, Tom 147, 154, 173
Krueger 164
Kurvers, Frank 162, 182
Kurvers, Leonard 119

Kurvers, Matthew 102
Kurvers, Mel 102
Kurvers, Nick 119
Kurvers Point Resort 102
Kurvers, Ted 119

L

Lake Ann 32, 102, 106, 117, 178
Lake Bavaria 15, 42, 86, 110
Lake Hazeltine 24, 26
Lake Lucy 32, 117
Lake Minnewashta
  29, 35, 103, 108, 109, 176
Lake Susan 42, 60, 102
Langdon, Harlow 40
Lawson, Larry 107
Leach, Alonzo 30
Leach, James 103
Leach's Resort 102, 103
Lette, Father 60
Lind, John 84
Livingston, Alexander 46
Livingston, John 46
Lotus Lake 102, 106, 165
Lubanski, Fr. Armand 186
Lubbe, Mary 76
Lyman, Adelle 29
Lyman, Arthur 85
Lyman, Henry
  24, 27, 28, 37, 40, 66, 68
Lyman, Mary 109, 176
Lyman, Richard 174

M

Maertz, John 14
Marschall, Joseph 140
Mason and Dimler General Store 71
Mason, Henry 71
Maurus, Anna 17
Maxwell 29
Maxwell, Fanny 35
Maxwell, William 45
Mayr, Father Magnus 60
McAllister, Earl 173
McArty, Timothy 37
Melchior, Delores 139
Mergens 9
Mergens, John 69
merger 176
Meuwissen 164
Meuwissen, Bob 160
Meuwissen, Howard 173
Meuwissen, Joe 79, 130, 131
Meuwissen, Susan 123, 137, 151
Miller, Frederick 18
Mingo, Rosemary Pauly 142, 143
Minnesota Horticultural Society
  85, 90, 171
Molnau 106
Moore, Joshua 24
Mudcura 96, 100
Murray, John 40

N

Nelson's Store 101
Nichols, Henry 20, 21, 22, 25, 28, 40
Nichols, Nancy 40
Northampton Colony 21, 35
Notermann, Arnold 43
Notermann, Maria 42
Nutting 20, 21, 22, 23, 24
Nutting, Freeman 20, 21
Nutting, Levi 21, 24
Nutting, Porter 21

O

Oswald, Father 162
Ottinger, Howard 111
Ottinger, Tobias 16, 85

P

Palmer, Paul 104, 111
Pauly, Abbie 76
Pauly, Albert 117, 124, 125
Pauly, Anna 71, 76
Pauly, Annie 125
Pauly, Christine 124
Pauly, Dutch
  115, 125, 138, 139, 162, 164
Pauly, Emil 105, 116, 117, 129
Pauly, Fritz 124
Pauly, Harry 139, 160, 167
Pauly, Henry 18, 60, 69
Pauly, Kenneth 142
Pauly, Kenny 105
Pauly, Michael 18
Pauly, Nick 71
Pauly, Roger 160
Pauly's 18
Pauly's 121, 122, 125
Pauly's Bar 129, 164
Pauly's Store 140, 141
Peter's Grove 101
Pine Grill 156
Pony Express Bar 131
Powers, George
  24, 28, 37, 40, 45, 55, 57
Prohibition 117

R

Rachel, Alexander 17
Railroad 118
Raser, Bogie 160
Raser, Elizabeth 76
Read, Stillman 37
Red Cedar Point 102
Redbirds 157, 158, 160, 161
Renz, Franz 14, 15, 37
Rettler, Donnie 169
Rettler, Elizabeth 71
Rettler, John 83
Rettler, Ray 136
Rettler, Rosella 71

Richardson, Ada Anding
  102, 108, 109, 176
Richardson, Irene 103
Riviera 164
Robertson, Bill 173
Roeser, Frank 115
Roeser, Leonard 83
Roeser, Lorraine
  114, 115, 125, 148, 151
Roeser, Martin 115
Roeser, Ron 147, 150, 160, 171, 176
Roeser, Roy 162
Roeser, Stan
  120, 138, 150, 151, 152, 158, 160
Rojina, Rita Meuwissen
  120, 133, 139, 140, 152, 171
Rose, Val 110
Rossbach, John 71
Rossbach, Minnie 71
Rossbach, Nicholas 57, 60
Rovers Club 110

S

Saint Hubert's Church
  61, 63, 73, 74, 118, 138, 142, 162, 186
Sarver, William 37, 40, 55
Schlenk, Anna 71
Schlenk, Jerry 170
Schlenk, Martin 71, 139
Schmid, Benedict 17, 33, 35, 36, 52
Schneider, Anton 119
Schneider, Bernie 167
Schneider, Engelbert 16, 51, 53
Schneider, Frank 160, 163
Schneider, Martin 37
Schneider, Matt 81
Schneider, Regina 76
Schroeder, Anna 76
Schroeder, Gerhard 71, 75
Schroeder, Peter 60
Schumman, John 119
Schutropp, Hank 137
Schutropp, Lawrence 122
Shaw, Joyce 108
Simmons, John 69
Sinnen, August 81, 115
Sinnen, Claude 139
Sinnen, Jean 172, 174
Snyder, Leon 172
State Bank of Chanhassen 133, 163, 182

T

Tanadoona 92, 94
Tessness, Adolph 169, 176, 177
Thompson, Jim 173
Thompson, Louise 152
Timmers, Mary 127
Tornado 169
Trumble, Israel 46
Trumble, Joel 28
Twin Cities Milk Producers Association
  105

V

Van Sloun, Florian 112
Village Hall 122, 186
Vinland 102
Vogel 15
Vogel, Anne 99
Vogel, August 16
Vogel, Claire 107
Vogel, Joseph 14, 16, 17, 37
Vogel, Magdalena 17
Vogel, Veronica 43

W

Weber, Fr. Firmin 163
Weller, Peter 60
Wilson, James 30
Wilson, Olive 30
Wilson, Willis 30, 110
Wood, Abel 28
Wood, Mary 44, 45
Wood, Mary Aspden 35
World War I 115
World War II 138
Wrase, Edna 111, 139
Wrase, Henry 108, 110, 111, 139, 176

Y

Yorkville 14, 28

Z

Zimmer, Bernard 71

Credits

Minnesota Historical Society

Paintings by Stanford Fennelle,
"Chanhassen, Evening" Cover
"Chanhassen" p. 155.
Painting of Lake Bavaria by Edwin Whitefield, p. 15

Chanhassen Dinner Theatre

photographs, p. 180.

Excelsior Historical Society

Diary of Benedict Schmid, translated by Edith Widmer.

Archdiocese of Saint Paul

photographs, p. 70

Saint Hubert's Church

photograph, p. 73

Acknowledgments

It has been my privilege throughout this project to work with an outstanding committee. Each member contributed wisdom, patience, and insight. Karen Engelhardt deserves special mention. Doug Fuller at The Press, Banta Corporation, assisted with the production of the book. This book was printed with financial assistance from The Press.

Staff at the Carver County Historical Society and the Minnesota Historical Society answered numerous questions and gave me guidance into their fine collections.

The oral history interviewers and transcribers accomplished outstanding work. They completed a training session, conducted more than fifty interviews, and then took the tapes and put them on paper. These interviews, combined with the collection of donated family papers and clippings, establish the centennial collection as the single major archive of Chanhassen history. All future historians will have to begin there.

Finally, this book would not have been possible without the people of Chanhassen.

Bibliographic Notes

There are few secondary sources to guide a researcher. Even the county history books make only a few references to the village and township. Probably the best summary to date is by Mary Lyman who gave a presentation to the Excelsior Reading Club in 1960.

The best primary resources are the Chaska and Excelsior newspapers but information is incidental and occasional. Some special subjects fare better. Mudcura was the subject of a talk by Susan Dreydoppel of the Carver County Historical Society. Noreen Roberts completed a National Register nomination form for the Fruit Breeding Farm that is on file with the State Historic Preservation Office. The SHPO files provide excellent source material on archaeological investigations triggered by federal and state preservation laws. There are also files on Village Hall and Saint Hubert's Church.

Primary resources are scattered. The Minnesota Historical Society holds the Nichols papers in their archives, including the letter in which Clarissa Cleaveland first uses the town's name. MHS has county and township records and state and federal census records on microfilm. Other special collections include the John Lind papers and the records of the Minnesota Horticultural Society. There are rather extensive records and oral history interviews concerning Elmer Kelm and the founding of the Democratic-Farmer-Labor Party. Other collections were useful. The staff at the Archives Department of the Archdiocese of St. Paul and Minneapolis were most helpful. The Carver County Historical Society maintains a collection of papers and photographs on Chanhassen history. They are in the midst of an indexing project for older county newspapers which should provide extremely valuable in the future. Camp Tanadoona has done a remarkable job of preserving their own history and are to be commended.

Selected References

Barac, Lavonne E. *Chaska: A Minnesota River City*. Minneapolis, 1976.

Bowen Ralph H. ed. and trans. *A Frontier Family in Minnesota: Letters of Theodore and Sophie Bost 1851-1920*. Minneapolis: University of Minnesota Press, 1981.

Diethelm, John A. *The History of St. Victoria Parish, 1857-1957*. St. Cloud: Sentinel Publishing Co., 1957.

Edwards, Everett E. and Horace Russell. "Wendelin Grimm and Alfalfa." *Minnesota History* 19, no. 2 (June 1938).

Herbst, Michele. "Chanhassen History." College Paper, Saint Thomas, 1983.

Lofstrom, Ted and Lynne VanBrocklin Spaeth. *Carver County: A Guide to Its Historic and Prehistoric Places*. St. Paul: Minnesota Historical Society, 1978.

Martens, Steven Cleo. "Ethnic Tradition and Innovation as Influences on Rural, Midwestern Building Vernacular: Findings From Investigations of Brick Houses in Carver County, Minnesota." Master's thesis, University of Minnesota, 1988.

Massman, John Casper. "German Immigration to Minnesota, 1850-1890." Ph. D. thesis, University of Minnesota, 1966.

Nichols, Charles W. "Henry Martyn Nichols and the Northampton Colony." *Minnesota History* 19, no. 2 (June 1938): 129-47.

Nichols, Charles W. "The Northampton Colony and Chanhassen." *Minnesota History* 20, no. 2 (June 1939): 140-5.

Nichols, Charles W. "Henry M. Nichols and Frontier Minnesota" *Minnesota History* 19, no. 3 (September 1938): 129-47.

Shannon, James P. *Catholic Colonization on the Western Frontier*. New Haven: Yale University Press, 1957.

Stephenson, George M. *John Lind of Minnesota*. Minneapolis: The University of Minnesota Press, 1935.

Chanhassen Centennial Book

Historical Committee

Ron Roeser
Beverly Gossard
Marlin Stene
Karen Engelhardt
Harold Kerber

Interviewers

Ron Roeser
Beverly Gossard
Marlin Stene
Cheryl Hobbs
Linda McGrath
Angie Marks
Kitty Sitter
Karen Engelhardt

Transcribers

Linda Bagley
Monica Poznick
Jean Steckling
Vicki Churchill
Kim Meuwissen
Nann Opheim
Shirlee Aus
Karen Engelhardt

Picture Scanning

David Hartley, Hartley Associates

Loaned Transcribing Machines

Loffler Business Communications
Chanhassen Secretarial Service

Printing

Doug Fuller, The Press, Banta Corporation

Mayor and City Council Members

Donald J. Chmiel, Mayor
Colleen Dockendorf, Councilwoman
Michael Mason, Councilman
Steven Berquist, Councilman
Mark Senn, Councilman
Don Ashworth, City Manager

This book was published with financial assistance from The Press, Banta Corporation.